Mariya Miteva

Study, Work and Travel in a Smart Way

AuthorHouse™ UK
1663 Liberty Drive
Bloomington, IN 47403 USA
www.authorhouse.co.uk
UK TFN: 0800 0148641 (Toll Free inside the UK)
UK Local: 02036 956322 (+44 20 3695 6322 from outside the UK)

Because of the dynamic nature of the Internet, any web addresses or links contained in this book may have changed
since publication and may no longer be valid. The views expressed in this work are solely those of the author and do
not necessarily reflect the views of the publisher, and the publisher hereby disclaims any responsibility for them.

Any people depicted in stock imagery provided by Getty Images are models,
and such images are being used for illustrative purposes only.
Certain stock imagery © Getty Images.

This book is printed on acid-free paper.

ISBN: 978-1-7283-5664-8 (sc)
978-1-7283-5663-1 (e)

Library of Congress Control Number: 2020916048

Print information available on the last page.

Published by AuthorHouse 11/30/2020

author HOUSE®

Study, Work, and Travel in a Smart Way

by

Mariya Miteva

Mariya

Around The Globe

ADVICE

INSIGHTS

GUIDELINES

ADVENTURES

RECOMMENDATIONS

INSPIRATIONAL LIFE TIPS

Contents

Dear Readers

I would like to share a surreal and mesmerizing story with you. The tale you are about to read is full of adventures, tips, and tricks, but most importantly it contains a handful of practical knowledge that you can use to build your own dream project to study, work, and travel around the globe with no personal budget, credit, and parental financial help. I hope it will inspire the genius in you and show you how to make your own dreams come true.

This narrative is suitable for those who are passionate and curious about studying, working, and traveling around the world but are perhaps unsure of how to go about it or whether it is indeed worth it. This may be due to a lack of clarity, confidence, or financial means. Whatever the reason or perceived barriers, here you can find concrete guidelines on how to build your own pathway by tapping into a completely new concept and methodology when considering and implementing your journey to a higher dimension.

In this book I document my journey around the globe and how I managed to accomplish so many extraordinary things, objectives that were believed to be out of my reach. I left home with €1,000 ($1,096) that I had earned from distribution flyers before leaving my hometown on the north coast of the Black Sea in Bulgaria.

Via my insights, practical knowledge, recommendations, and philosophy, I promise to inspire and give you the means to make your dreams come true with no personal capital. I'll show you how to build your own dream project without huge sums of money behind you. I hope you enjoy the read!

Mariya

Around The Globe

Introduction

Everybody knows how to deal with happiness and embrace abundance, and most of us would accept with excitement the possibility of traveling to foreign lands in a constructive way. If this is valid for you too, please keep reading! In this book, you'll learn how to:

- transform difficult moments in life into tremendous opportunities;

- create abundance solely by having the right mindset;

- tune your mind filter to perceive a silver lining behind every cloud; and

- travel and study in the most prestigious universities around the world with no budget, credits, student loans, or parental financial help.

If you want to find out how all that is possible, then this book is for you.

In order to enjoy the read and follow my tips and tricks, the answers to the following questions need to be yes:

- Do you like to play?

- Do you like to travel?

- Do you like to study? That is, do you like to learn new subjects?

- Are you curious?

On a side note, do you have a budget? No? Even better!

Students with access to capital will take a different path to the one I took. By not possessing wealth, I was forced to develop my own senses in order to access my dreams. So if you truly want to awaken your genius, push yourself in order to find your own solutions, and trigger your imagination, there is no place for capital. To apply my concept of how to study, work, and travel around the globe in a smart way, you don't need a budget, savings, or sponsors, but you do need to have the courage, discipline, and will to learn that will help you pass the levels to qualify for the next adventure. Your attitude and abilities to overcome the challenges we encounter in everyday life will turn you in to a truly privileged young adult.

Welcome to this introduction to a new philosophy, mindset, and belief system in respect of how to study, work, and travel in a smart way, accomplished by embracing problems we all detest and turning them into gold mines. In this book, I showcase how to identify which challenges are worth the battle and how to detect the ones that are not. Inconveniencies, difficulties, and obstacles are my playground, which I characterize as a special place where I perform and outperform. Most people in my shoes would get annoyed and leave the battlefield, thus leaving plenty of room to maneuver without hardly any competition at all. The time has come. Here you can learn how to face all kinds of issues, use them as a resource, convert them into opportunities, and finally profit from them.

Do you want to learn how to juggle and overcome life's puzzles in a spectacular way? I can show you how to start seeing obstacles as unique life moments and why you should stop avoiding the challenges imposed by our society but rather face them head-on! Both obstacles and challenges are there for a reason, to allow you to shine brighter amongst the crowd once you have passed them. Don't be scared or afraid. You can do it. You can overcome them. You just don't know it yet.

Read This Book and Build Your Own Dream Project!

Here, I share my concept and methods on how to build a project around studying, working, and traveling around the globe. For those of you who desire an alternative life, I am about to unveil a nonlinear approach that I trialed. This method is for those who wish to have access to an education and dream to travel to foreign places yet have no money to afford such unrealistic adventures, hence my alternative approach "in a smart way." I'm writing this story for all of you that have big dreams.

I would like to give voice to a new philosophy, a different vision, and practical guidance in order to trigger your imagination and ideas and hopefully inspire you to make your dreams come true. Now is the time to start building!

Summary

This book tells an inspirational true story. The protagonist is called Mariya, who wanted to study in the most prestigious universities around the world. She wanted to travel around the globe, learn languages, and meet new cultures but had no money to do so. And her parents had no budget. Applying for a student credit was not an option, and there was no sponsor to finance any of those utopic, unrealistic dreams.

So at the age of eighteen, Mariya rolled up her sleeves and worked through the summer, distributing flyers in the seaside resorts in Bulgaria. With the money made, Mariya took a thirty-hour bus journey to France, saying goodbye to family and childhood friends from a dusty bus station in post-communist Bulgaria.

Mariya juggled university life with student jobs, found her way to Brazil to study in the most prestigious university in South America, traveled with no limits, and learned to speak fluent Portuguese. She found a pathway to an internship as a lifeguard in the United States while working simultaneously in a media company and bartending in a fancy sushi restaurant in downtown Chicago. Yet this was just the beginning.

Via the free university system and the help of the French state, Mariya embarked on a shiny new journey to sunny Mexico, where she learned to speak fluent Spanish and to dance salsa. She subsequently landed a place at the mythical Sorbonne University in Paris. She then went on to find a well-paid, high-profile job in breathtaking Switzerland until London called, and the journey continues there today.

Yet it all started with vast and unrealistic dreams combined with the determination and will to learn. This got Mariya from distributing flyers on the beach to traveling around the globe and making every single utopic dream come true.

Some of you may stop at the stage where "my parents cannot afford any of these activities," so the idea is to inspire young adults and parents that anything is possible if you set an intention with your heart and soul and then of course back it up with hard work and the right decisions, while remaining aware of new opportunities and learning to go with a new type of flow.

This book contains advice, insights, guidelines, adventures, recommendations, and inspirational life tips. Read this book and build your own dream project!

About Mariya

Welcome to my world! I have documented my adventures so I can share my methods, tips, and tricks with you, which all allowed me to take myself from my hometown in Bulgaria on the North Black Sea coast to over fifty different countries around the world. This was not before gaining a higher education in France. I then went on to study in Brazil, the United States, and Mexico before returning to deploy my newfound skills in Switzerland.

Via my insights, practical knowledge, recommendations, and philosophy, I promise to inspire you and give you the means to make your dreams come true, even when your path is not clear or your bank account is not full. In fact, it's better if it's empty, and I will tell you why.

Should you be aspiring to study and work abroad, I would like to assist in pointing you in the right direction, to travel anywhere you wish to go within an organized and approved setting. In sharing my experiences, I hope to motivate you into understanding that your willpower is everything and money is just an accessory. I spend as much time as I can traveling. I centered most of my wanderlust on studying, working, and learning new languages. I can now speak French, English, Portuguese, Spanish, and Russian. So I hope you'll find all you need in my reflections of how to *Study, Work, and Travel in a Smart Way*.

In documenting my adventures, I have three objectives:

1. I often come across inspiring quotes on my social media platforms, intended to motivate me when I am going through a difficult patch. You too? I'm addressing all of you who need some positive vibes taken from my short stories that I have collected from around the globe. I will share a slightly different philosophy, hopefully some new knowledge, and a few tricks I discovered when juggling nonlinear scenarios abroad. My aim is to give you insights on how you can deliver huge projects funded by minimal personal budgets. This requires maximum organization and a greater awareness of your potential and environment. The following chapters should inspire you and give you the means to believe in yourself and help you grasp your freedom and generate new energy. For this reason, I have selected the recounted events with due care, aiming to showcase how important it is to plant the seed, set your intention, stay focused on your dream, wait patiently, and then enjoy the generous harvest.

I'm living proof that even the funkiest dreams are achievable, in conjunction with those inspirational quotes, which materialize in the physical world. How? Read on and see in the next episodes. I will demonstrate how unrealistic wishes, utopic ambitions, and childhood dreams can come true if you live according to Einstein's belief that "logic will get you from A to B, imagination can take you everywhere."

The message I want to convey is that a lack of financial resources or family financial support should not obstruct you or force you to give up because it's possible to make big things happen without a large budget. Your heart, awareness, discipline, and willingness to learn will get you through. One of the major driving forces to this is curiosity. As Uncle Alfred said, "I have no special talent. I am only passionately curious."

I believe in the English proverb, "If there is a will, there is a way." In my story, I explain how, against many odds, I continuously fed my curiosity, which allowed me to travel around the globe in a smart way. Now it's your turn, so try to feed your curiosity and share your experiences too!

2. I'm addressing future university students who want to study abroad and are ideally willing to learn new languages. I have documented how I prepared two exchange programs in Brazil and Mexico. Moreover, my readers in the university age range may find a few tricks and hints on how to do an internship in the United States. Again, I'm hoping that in reading my articles, you will learn how to work and travel around the globe in a smart way and rely on yourself. My wish is to give ideas to future or current university students how to activate and synchronize a multitude of potential financial resources and remind you about simple tools that, when combined, give you the power to juggle an exciting and fruitful life to your best ability.

Bear in mind, both concept and methodology (chapter 2) remain the same. I have personally checked their effectiveness and classified them for my readers today. If you need my help, feel free to contact me for advice.

In order to facilitate your *voyage* ("trip" in French) in this book, please find a bit more guidance on how to navigate in this text. In "The Structure behind the Shiny Vitrine," I provide concrete guidelines on how to build your plan of action and sponsor it, giving you tips and trick as well as a detailed guidance through life lessons, lots of practical information (e.g., scholarships plus other financial resources), precious advice, and quality nourishment for your imagination.

I am showcasing how it works and what it looks like when the concept of "Layer within the Layer 'Mise en abyme'" is applied in real life. "I like to compare my method with that of painters' centuries ago, proceeding from layer to layer," said Alberto Moravia.

In "As Above So Below," (like in the spiritual world), when working on a project, count and consider three levels below, making sure the surface above, which you climb on, is a platform with steady pillars.

3. This read is also suitable for parents who might want to know more about how student life works when your kids want to study abroad, although you as parents are not sponsoring the adventure. I hope to reassure parents that the road I am illustrating is safe, the targets are feasible, and it is indeed healthy to let your child embark on such an adventure and sail the boat to a higher realm.

Life is a playground, and my golden rule is not let a lack of money or savings block you. It is very important to stay focused and disciplined and believe in yourself. To assist in reassuring you and to prove that anything is possible, I am giving you concrete and mesmerizing examples where things happened as if by magic, extracted directly from a true story, which I documented in the episodes about Brazil, the United States, Mexico, Paris, Switzerland, London, and Bulgaria.

If you like the read, feel free to follow me on Instagram at *mariya_atg*, and if you wish to see more, I will do my best to share my current adventures with you. I will be broadcasting from London to you soon.

The Structure behind the Shiny Vitrine

Chapter 1. Overview, Profile, and Philosophy

People who say it cannot be done should not interrupt those who are doing it.

—George Bernard Shaw[1]

Overview

I intend to give you hints, tips, and tricks on how you can finance your studies, partially through university scholarships and state help and in combination with part-time student jobs while living quite comfortably. Throughout the chapters, I will explain how you can activate and synchronize a multitude of financial resources while reminding you about simple tools that have the power to enable you to make the most of life.

My story goes like this. Born and raised in Bulgaria, I started my bachelor's degree in France at a public university in Lyon in the mid-2000s and later graduated at the Sorbonne University in Paris. Meanwhile, and partially thanks to a compilation of scholarships, I managed to engineer, then to finance two projects of mine that allowed me to attend two exchange programs at the University of São Paulo in Brazil and the Universidad Autónoma del Estado de Mexico in Mexico. I also did an internship in media and film production in Chicago, United States, while lifeguarding on the weekends. These projects were funded with a minimum personal budget, thus with maximum organization and great awareness.

Throughout my journey, I learned to speak a myriad of languages fluently (French, Portuguese, Spanish, English, and Russian) and traveled restlessly around the globe thanks to my hard work at school and outside as well as the financial help from the French state combined with student scholarships. Shortly after I graduated from the Sorbonne in Paris, an international company in Switzerland recruited me, where I spent six wonderful years working in the industry I always dreamed to be a part of. I recently moved to the United Kingdom to embark on a new career adventure. You can follow me on Instagram at *mariya_atg* if you wish to see more about this.

Now I will describe the approach I applied before I finished high school. I had an enormous desire to continue my studies in France and travel the world, but my parents could not afford to meet my expectations or my requirements. At the age of eighteen, I had no income to cover the costs myself. Unfortunately most kids in my shoes would stop there and not investigate alternative options, due to an obvious lack of financial resources.

Wrong approach! You don't have to fit in the box if you don't like it because you can design your own box. Remember, you are indeed in control of yourself. Don't let your financial situation or lack of financial support block you because it is possible to make big things happen with a small budget.

---

[1] "George Bernard Shaw (1856 – 1950) - an Irish playwright, novelist, critic and politician, awarded the Nobel Prize in Literature in 1925" (Biography)

A Summary of the Journey So Far on the World Map

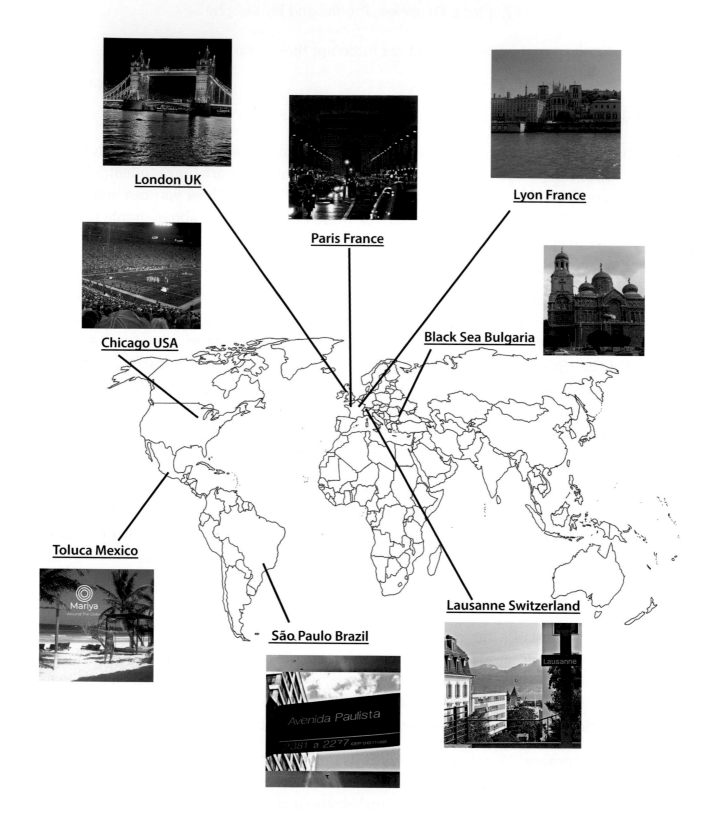

London UK

Paris France

Lyon France

Chicago USA

Black Sea Bulgaria

Toluca Mexico

São Paulo Brazil

Lausanne Switzerland

Profile

I was born in Bulgaria in the 1980s during the communist period, which doesn't mean that I grew up not eating bananas or not knowing the taste of Coca-Cola. However, I certainly didn't have access to many of the life improvement materials, means, and information a kid growing up in Western Europe had. I believe many of you coming from countries with a developing economy can relate to this situation.

Nevertheless, I was always in an unapologetically ambitious mood. I had access to my dreams, to unrealistic visions for a kiddo who had never seen the world outside her hometown. The story I am about to tell you is not fiction. It is not a movie script (yet). Maybe there will be a Netflix Original TV series upgrade. Anything is possible. It's about how to survive in the big, wide world far from your comfort zone.

By sharing this story with you, I hope to inspire and motivate those of you who have big ambitions. Ideally you should have some language abilities or an interest in developing them. But you don't need capital to finance studies or travels, and you must not fear a challenge. It is possible to embark on a shiny journey, an epic and rewarding adventure with minimum personal savings, if you plan your project carefully and execute it to your best ability.

I studied in a trilingual high school with an enhanced focus on French as a first language and English as a second language. After I graduated from high school in the mid-2000s, I left Bulgaria with the total amount of €1,000 ($1,094.85) in my pocket, earned from distributing flyers in nearby beach resorts.

In September of the same year, I arrived at my destination, determined I would make it happen and pursue my superior education in France, where I was accepted to study media and communications at a local free state university in the city of Lyon. I was fully aware that I needed to think fast and be smart about every move I made, as I could barely cover the costs even for the first few months.

Studying in prestigious institutions in France, Brazil, and Mexico and travelling around the world was perceived as pure utopia at that stage. Nevertheless, I rolled up the sleeves and started sponging any information my mind could absorb. I filtered it and kept it. Further down the line, I finally managed to finance my first project to study in Lyon and found two part-time student jobs, and the rest followed.

As I mentioned, the universities I went to are examples, extracted from my own story. In your situation, you will have to identify what your university options are based on your inspirations and find the equivalent. Again, approach and methodology both remain the same; therefore this is what you should be tapping into to tailor and adapt your project. To save you time and energy, I will share the channels I discovered along my journey.

Philosophy

Life is a playground, and my golden rule is not to let a lack of money or savings for an education block you. Studying—and moreover studying abroad—should not be perceived as a right reserved for privileged children whose parents' duty is to supposedly pay their tuition fees and cover the costs of living. If you follow that well-beaten path, you may just skip out on going to the university of life, which has more value than any fancy diploma issued by a well-renowned institution.

When do you go to the university of life? Often when your parents cannot afford to sponsor your fantasy studies and even less your travels. It is not their duty either. Thus, you must become creative and financially resourceful in your approach of how to live the best time of your life without ending up on a survival camp during the execution of this exciting life project. It is important to understand and establish your intention to kick-start the plan, to visualize it, and then to start going, and by going, I mean going with the flow, as it is essential to keep yourself in the flow. By flow, I mean to attach yourself to a structure with stable pillars and then to remain alert about what this structure offers.

To build my structure, I chose the university as an institution; a stable long-term student job; and a charming, shared flat with reliable roommates and friends, situated right above the bar where I worked throughout my entire stay in Lyon, France.

The Structure behind the Shiny Vitrine

Chapter 2. Concept and Organization Methods

For every minute spent organizing, an hour is earned.

—Benjamin Franklin[2]

In the following chapter, I will share with you the steps and methodology I applied to enroll at a public university in Lyon, France, where I studied information and communications (the basis of journalism and media).

In order to prepare myself, I researched some carefully selected public universities in France. I suggest avoiding Paris at the start of your adventure or any megapolis, for that matter. I based my selection on a deduction of all major subjects related to heavier disciplines such as medicine, engineering, mathematics, IT, or law. So I focused on choosing a major amongst the available options in the human and social sciences disciplines.

I selected a university in the city of Lyon that offered a major in information and communication, the base for journalism and media studies. I chose English linguistics as a secondary major. I paid about €300 ($328.48) for the whole university year, including a basic but good health insurance. The current tuition fees in 2020–2021 remain symbolic.

The education programs in the human and social sciences are usually less heavy and significantly lighter in terms of workload and number of classes per week compared to degrees in medicine, engineering, IT or law. Unfortunately we need to remain realistic and keep the right balance, so even if deep down you want to study law, for example, it will be harder to do without any capital, and the workload is obviously significantly heavier.

So you must adjust your aspirations and trim them into a down-to-earth realistic possibility (should the desire to travel supersede that of becoming a barrister), that is, information, communication, English linguistics, economy, management, marketing, political science, psychology, sociology, and so on.

For my type of project, you will need free time to work outside of your university timetable in order to finance your studies and sustain yourself by your own means. Yes, there will be scholarships within your reach, but you still need to work part time. You have two hands and a head on your shoulders. Trust me, this is a very resourceful start.

The beauty of the exercise is that you need to find a flexible part-time job, which allows you to combine it with your university schedule. Potential jobs you need to target are waitressing,

---

[2] "Benjamin Franklin (1705 – 1790) - an American polymath and one of the Founding Fathers of the United States" (Biography)

bartending, housekeeping, babysitting, moving furniture, and so forth. It is for you to design this part of the adventure; it is the easiest part.

In any event, you need to find a part-time job as soon as you arrive in the host country/ city. Once again, the student job you target and opt for must be flexible and compatible with your school schedule. It is mandatory. Believe me, such jobs do exist. You can find them on the web or via the traditional way of distributing résumés/CVs in bars and restaurants.

Remember, it is important to have a well-compacted journey between your university and your place of work in order to save time and energy between commutes, so it is important to have all three domains (school, work, and home) strategically selected location-wise, and yes, this is possible to achieve. Also, I will be honest with you, indeed you will need to rely on leftovers of time to study and provide quality homework but it is possible to achieve to if you respect the guidelines. Depending on how fast you incorporate information, might have to consider studying while taking the public transport for example. I never underestimated these bits of time I had for myself, while using the public transport. It helped me learn how to focus in any type of surrounding and reconsider, rethink if I could afford to be distracted. I couldn't, so these twenty minutes metro ride meant one chapter read, processed and retained. This exercise was repeated on daily basis. It worked out well for me.

Student job-wise, if I were you, I would avoid jobs at nightclubs and/or work that involves you being online. If you want to be a digital nomad one day, great! You will have all your time to do become an influence, but now don't skip the opportunity to study first.

Contrary to what people think, having one or two part-time jobs will only contribute to your overall life balance. It won't make it harder. Studying and working simultaneously will help you channel your energy and use every bit of your time carefully and constructively. Working twenty to twenty-five hours a week and studying twenty to twenty-five hours a week is affordable as well as physically and mentally rewarding, especially for healthy people between the ages of eighteen to twenty-five.

Don't get scared! You don't need your parents' financial support! Remember, there are repercussions to this option. Having access to external financial help from a family source can spoil you. It could easily prevent you from growing up and becoming more mature. It won't push you to go out of your comfort zone, and if you stay there, you will find no growth in this safe place. Reciprocally, there is no comfort in the growing process either.

What do I mean by repercussions? Well, you would impose natural boundaries inhibiting your exposure to learn the language of the host country you live in, as you would, when you are completely immersed in a working environment. The way you would explore the world around you would be very different because with this type of ready-to-consume financial help, you would naturally choose your cozy place of comfort and adopt a low-risk attitude. It is not only detrimental, but also beneficial to go outside of your comfort zone, between the age of eighteen and twenty-three, in order to build your network, shape your mindset, and become an open-minded person and individual thinker.

Don't feed your laziness by conveniently believing that it's your parents' obligation to pay your education and living costs. Now is the time to let your creativity get to work, demystify the powers of your nonlinear mind you would most likely develop, and continue nourishing it over time by being tuned to this style of consciousness.

Don't get distracted by the illusion that only privileged kids can have access to the best universities in the world and travel the globe restlessly. You can do it too. However, you must plan it better than some. In the planning process, you will become more creative and develop a great awareness of all-surrounding social and financial elements and opportunities. All of it plays a considerable role in the newly designed structure of this brand-new ecosystem of yours, which I just gave you a glimpse of.

Working while studying will actually help you build a network. You need a stable network in the new host country, as you cannot be a solo player. You will always need people's help in certain situations, so it's better to embrace this from the get-go. Now is the time to really start working on building a whole new ecosystem around you by making friends via four main channels: university, work (colleagues and customers, if applicable), flatmates (as you will most likely have to live in a shared flat for a while), and friends of friends.

As a bonus, there are recreational activities. Yes, it is highly likely that you will have time left over for some recreational activities, if you organize yourself well.

Layer within the Layer "Mise en Abyme"

Chapter 3. University versus City: Research and Preparation

I don't love studying. I hate studying. I like learning. Learning is beautiful.

—Natalie Portman[3]

Start researching public universities before the last year of high school because in this last year, you need to have made up your mind and choices as well as be ready to submit (ideally) a minimum of three applications per school at three different universities. Type "List of French universities" in your browser (or *"liste des universités françaises"* in French). Hereafter, you will find guidance on how to filter the disciplines you are interested in, regarding the universities that have attracted your attention, and then how to choose the city to live in.

Approach 1: City versus University

Compile a list of cities you feel you resonate with, where you either have friends who can help you in the beginning or a city you fell in love with. Honestly speaking, you need to like the host city where you will ideally be spending the next few crucial years of your life, and you need to consider this when you make your selections. You need to embrace the new environment; therefore, you must deliberately like it in order to avoid possible resistance in the adjustment period or any type of culture shock that can shake up you, your school project, or even your health.

Approach 2: University versus City

Let's assume that you have no preferences toward the city or the climate is not an issue for you and your sole and only priority is the major you are about to enroll in. To be fair, I believe this is secondary because if you research any of the lighter disciplines I mentioned earlier, you will soon find out that those are offered in most universities in all big cities. Popular majors such as economy, management, marketing, psychology, sociology, and so forth are instituted in any social and human sciences-dedicated university of quality.

Ideally you should find a combination of both: city plus university. You don't want to feel like you are compromising the city that you pick to the detriment of the university of your choice, as there could be repercussions further down the line. My priority has always been that I need to feel comfortable in my new environment, and this approach has always served me well. Therefore, deciding on the city should go first and then the university and discipline will follow. All will fall into place naturally.

---

[3] "Natalie Portman (1981) - an actress and filmmaker with dual Israeli and American citizenship" (Biography)

After you have researched and prepared a list of universities, select the major you want to apply for on the website by clicking on "Education" ("*Formations*" in French), for example, "information and communication." Then click on "application and enrollment" ("*candidature et inscription*" in French). Check and prepare the required documents you need to fill in to submit your multiple applications for the major(s) of your choice.

I have prepared an example of a list of potential documents, usually required by the universities, to give you an idea of the file you need to prepare and submit.

NB!

- Bear in mind that there are deadlines. Do not miss them!

- Each university and major will ask for different sets of documents to prepare your application file.

- You will always need to present a cover letter. If you want to consult the cover letters I used in French, English, Portuguese, Spanish, and Russian throughout my journey, Click here or go to matg.co.uk

The following examples are lists of university-required documents (to be translated in French):

- Curriculum vitae (CV/résumé)

- Diploma from high school, featuring your grades statement, and any other relevant diploma(s)

- Diploma or certificate stating your level of mastery of the French language (for foreigners)

  ○ Double-check with the university of your choice that they do accept the diploma you can provide.

- The specific university form stating the disciplines you have chosen

- ID or passport

- Student card (eventually)

- ID photo

- Other specific documents

The Structure behind the Shiny Vitrine

Chapter 4. Tips and Tricks to Studying Abroad

Layer by layer, art strips life bare.

—Robert Musil[4]

The French state (via the Crous organism) provides scholarships not only to French, but also to foreign students from the (European Union/European Economic Area) Switzerland with low family incomes who study at public institutions in France. When you select the country where you want to study, it is important to consider the global-social approach of the government toward higher education. That is, the United Kingdom, the Netherlands, and the United States are not the best destinations for this type of project. Your target is to study in a country where the university's tuition is symbolic, that is, average tuition fees of 100 to 500 euros/dollars per year or entirely free.

Moreover, once you have been accepted in the university that is right for you and after you validate your first year, assuming that you qualify, of course, you could have access to several cumulative scholarships, giving you the means to go to one or even two student exchange programs. There is a whole new layer of options and possibilities ahead of you after you accomplish the first step, which is to get accepted to study any light major or discipline in a public university.

After accomplishment and validation of your first year, called License 1 or L1, from your three-year bachelor's degree, opportunity number two comes into play. I am now turning your attention to explore the possibility of embarking on a student exchange program abroad. If you are willing to invest some time exploring your options, then I recommend it. I suggest that you go to the international relations department, which any university has in some form, or other in order to search what suitable exchange programs are being offered. Most universities have a solid portfolio of agreements with foreign universities for exchange students. The benefits from these programs are tremendous in terms of exposure to different cultures, foreign languages, global knowledge, and personal development.

Based on the feedback you are given at the international relations department, start preparing your file to apply for a university exchange program of your choice. Bear in mind though that the major and respective subjects you choose should remain the same as the one you have enrolled in at your home university. If you study communications, you need to select a host university that offers the same major. It is not possible to switch to law, for example, during the year or semester abroad.

---

[4] "Robert Musil (1880 – 1942) - an Austrian philosophical writer" (Biography)

The procedure on how to apply for a scholarship to study abroad will be part of the file you will need to learn how to prepare and submit on time. The best source of information is the international relations department, which each institution has in some form. To learn more about the exact process, steps, and mindset to build this layer, please refer to chapter 7. For more information regarding the scholarships, read chapter 8.

NB!

Different regions (or departments) in France offer different university exchange program scholarships, "bourse de mobilité internationale." For example, in Auvergne-Rhône-Alpes, these scholarships are amongst the highest in the country.

The international relations department will provide you with insights on how to research the best place to study. The beauty of this program is that you continue to pay the tuition to your home university and not the tuition of the host university abroad.

Let's assume that you play your cards well. You can end up studying in a very expensive, fancy, and prestigious university in the United States, for example, during the semester or year abroad. The emphasis is that now you know about this option, you can think about adding a second or even a third layer to your education, which I like to call "Mise en Abyme" from the French, meaning "Layer within the Layer."

- Layer 1: Normal study in university

- Layer 2: Exchange program 1

- Layer 3: Exchange program 2

I am showcasing how it works and what it looks like when my concept of "Mise en Abyme" is applied in real life. Click on the links below to visit my journey through the student exchange programs in Brazil and Mexico. Like the spiritual world and philosophies, when working on a project, count and consider three levels below to make sure that the surfaces, or platforms, you step on are steady and sturdy pillars. Consider three levels below to make sure the levels above are steady when you climb up on them, not for when you climb down on them. Be honest with yourself!

In order to facilitate building your pillars, I believe it is paramount to aim high and broad. The high is the moon, which is the equivalent to your target institution, the institution you believe you want to study at. "Broad" means basically aiming to land among the stars, which is the equivalent to the next best thing, and potentially being accepted to study at your third-choice university, which, trust me, is perfectly fine. Oftentimes we work with a catalog of targets inspired by sometimes unclear ideas, superficial knowledge, and/or someone else's experiences that are not necessarily relevant for us. Be confident that the universe often knows better than us, is wiser, and will dispatch us to a better place than the one we pictured or planned, so trust the outcome of the work you have put in. The results will be generous!

Always bear in mind that once you have built your platform on stable pillars, only then can you travel around the globe constructively, backed by the financial support of the generous structure in the socially oriented country you have selected. Speaking of the platform, feel free to check chapter 7 to know exactly what to do and when.

To be clear, I have no intention to life-mentor you my dear readers or share with you the next groundbreaking strategy, combined with special techniques, on how to change and straighten out anybody's life or mind. Although I do intend to unveil certain tracks that may well upgrade your well-being and/or the future of your children, should a parent be reading this? I am giving you a template with guidelines, which you can follow step by step. Bear in mind that the template is tapping into one of the most important pillars of your conscious life, studying.

As Above So Below

Chapter 5. A Myriad of Languages

One who speaks only one language is one person, but one who speaks two languages is two people.

—Turkish proverb

Languages have always fascinated me. This passion of mine was maybe the biggest driving force and the main thread in my life. At the age of four, I had my first conscious encounter with a foreign language by watching "The Cop from Saint-Tropez" ("*Le gendarme de Saint-Tropez*" in French) on the television. I was so enthralled by the divine sounds that Louis de Funès was making that I felt this incredible urge to reproduce, imitate, or copy, if you wish, the same string of tinkly, bizarre, and unknown sounds, music to my ears, called French. My parents couldn't understand this fascination of mine.

Widely perceived and well known that the French language is a complex linguistic skill, I was advised that it wouldn't be a good fit for me to spend my energy on it. Have you ever had that moment with your parents? Maybe in a different context, but the idea is overall the same.

I am sharing this with you, as you will see in the following episodes, how expansive this moment was in the story. Then I invite you to appraise what this determination meant to a four-year-old. I believe many of you can relate to it. I am giving you the proof that it is worth investing time into building your dream too. You can follow firsthand how this moment provoked someone to set a goal, visualize a path, and specify a life pattern that led to the completion of this goal.

Early 2000s: High School

In my high school years, I studied French (first language) and English (second language). I believed I was on the right path. I had a set intention in my conscious life that started in childhood. In high school, not only did I gain all the techniques that enabled me to learn French, but I also received the good Bulgarian free state education, which enabled me to procure a sturdy template of how any Latin-based language worked, which came in handy much later. You will see when and how I had to reach out and build the actual pillars through the tough structure of the grammatical and phonetic behavior of any Romanic language. This in turn lifted my energy and enabled me to grasp Portuguese and Spanish in a matter of weeks.

The rest of the school subjects hardly mattered except for French and English, accompanied by history and geography. (Surprise! Surprise!) Mariya already knew that she wanted to travel the world to see these historic monuments and places we learned about in high school; however, we had no real financial means to touch base and experience these things as Eastern European high school students.

Throughout my educational process, I was introduced to the French culture and the existence of the mythical University of the Sorbonne in Paris. This is where, according to my French history classes, all philosophers were trained. Logically, to become one of them, you must go to the Sorbonne, if that's where they all come from there, right? I was so fascinated by this mesmerizing world of knowledge and concentration of intelligence that my teachers painted. Exactly, as you can guess, the Sorbonne was Mariya's next goal.

In order to follow in similar steps, you will need to know or be willing to learn French and/or German, Spanish, Italian, or Portuguese, for example. The Scandinavian languages work too. The above languages are real axes, linked to the social orientation of their respective countries, translated into scholarships and fruitful soil in the material world.

If you know or want to learn English only, this approach would simply limit your options, to the extent that you won't be able to reap all of the benefits, accrued by infiltrating and befriending other cultures and languages, as well as associating yourself with the local population by embracing those things.

It is possible that this language resource is not enough to accomplish such a project, and speaking only English will not take you very far in a journey like the one Mariya undertook. Reciprocally, without decent English, you would be blocked too. The key is to be curious. "I have no special talent. I am only passionately curious," said Albert Einstein.

If you have language abilities and/or are curious enough to develop them, believe me, it is worth investing time before the age of twenty-five to learn at least one other European language. The knowledge of such a communication tool will get you a long way and prepare you for later in life. Beyond the age of twenty-five, when you will most likely start your professional career, you will not have that quality time with your mind at your disposal to dedicate the incorporation of new vocabulary. You will lose the once-upon-a-time sense of play with grammar, the learning process will be perceived as a burden, and the learning curve will be nowhere near what you were used to before the age of twenty-five. Trust me.

I tried it with Russian some years later, Russian being the closest relative to my mother tongue, and the outcome was quite different compared to the French, Portuguese, or Spanish language learning process I undertook before the age of twenty-five, which was much easier!

There are also multiple layers to be observed within the linguistic universe. A lot of benefits are overlooked. When I am in doubt, I don't just leave it out. I like the saying from Charles Bukowski, "The problem with the world is that intelligent people are full of doubt, while the stupid people are full of confidence."

Due to my lack of confidence, I would naturally check and filter six times the knowledge I have access to through my language abilities to find a satisfactory answer, allowing me to study and track the different cultural alignments and belief systems attached to any linguistic capacity or faculty.

I have found that the same information overlaps across different languages/cultures, sampled from three language families: Latin (French, Portuguese, and Spanish), Germanic (English), and Slavic (Bulgarian and Russian). Sometimes, believe it or not, I come across huge discrepancies in both, the culture and the belief system, for something as silly as dumping used coffee in the sink.

For example, the Spanish say it's good for the plumbing system, while the French say the same action blocks the pipes. The illustrated discrepancies have a smaller impact, but if you change and amplify the context, the impact is tremendous.

People overlook that potential and underestimate the power of that cultural and belief system, which comes as part of the linguistic package. I don't know why people are fascinated by the fact that someone is able to speak six languages fluently, a person who can reproduce and convey the same message multiplied by six, like a parrot. I don't see why this is so fascinating. Do you know why? Please enlighten me!

The core value is the cultural references, in my opinion. The fact that you can relate to a certain population and source unique knowledge directly from the origin has much more value. Don't you think?

Have you ever thought about the fact that languages are actually a brilliant intellectual investment? I mean grammar and vocabulary, both components forming the main ecosystem of any language, hardly evolve in a lifetime. While the structure and algorithms of all social media platforms tend to constantly change and evolve, languages are a rather stagnant material. Once you learn the grammatical structure, the skeleton, and then you form the body by incorporating a good amount of relevant vocabulary, you are good to go for a lifetime. Neither the grammar nor the vocabulary will ever change shades in a tremendous way, causing you to have to relearn a language. Once you understand how to decode a language, in a matter of weeks (in cases of a complete immersion), then you only have one thing to worry about, to keep the knowledge fresh and constantly updated. You need to make friends to talk to. This is the trick, and it is mandatory. This is the place where everything starts and ends, when you deal with a linguistic communication tool. You have to feed it on a constant basis; otherwise it dies indeed. There is no workaround, my dears, trust me.

Languages are a great lifetime investment; however in order to avoid letting your linguistic assets become rusty, you will need to organize your everyday life and overall lifestyle, revolving around constant exposure and access to the respective set of languages. This comes naturally, believe me.

To keep up your linguistic powers, you will naturally train yourself to detect exposure to the specific cultural environment that the language you resonate with is attached to. The more you progress, the more you will feel the need to dig deeper in developing your linguistic faculty. It may seem a burden as you are reading this, but it is not and will not be. Just let yourself go and start meeting new people.

What do you think? Do you like the idea? Can you picture yourself juggling three or four languages simultaneously? Of course you can. I don't have special abilities, but I achieved this without taking this for granted. So why can't you? The trick is to be passionately curious. There is no other enigma.

As Above So Below

Chapter 6. The Notion of Time

Time isn't the main thing. It's the only thing.

—Miles Davis[5]

"The notion of time and the illusion, that we have time, falls under the category of our biggest mistakes, and misconceptions," said Buddha. "Time flies, but you are the pilot, don't forget about it," said Michael Altshuler. Optimize your time in the framework you design for yourself. Money comes and goes. Time doesn't. Which one is more valuable?

Through this case study, inspired by a true story, I am providing you with knowledge on how to build pillars. Pillar one (sleeping/inactive) and pillar two (working/active) consist of generating energy and money. To have quality sleep, you need to organize your journeys well, and to get the dream job, you will most likely need to back up your project with the relevant study program. The third most precious pillar of your own conscious life is studying.

I have come across many compelling messages, conveyed in holistic ways to coach us on how to change our life pattern, in order to start living a nice, simple, linear life, full of light and happiness. But how about accepting the fact that life isn't linear and cannot be this way if you are not offered such possibilities by default? Once used to dealing with nonlinear scenarios, you will get bored if things roll out in a linear way like with other people because your mindset and flow of your thoughts would not surrender since you always had to build and break down life puzzles. Then make peace with that fact and use it to your advantage in a practical way, being fully aware of the precious time you have. It is all yours to make the most of!

To balance yourself emotionally, try to identify, if you don't know yet, what type of timeless resource makes your heart beat and feeds your soul. What do I mean by timeless resource? The sea, mountains, special places, activities, or sights we like to see and spend time at represent such resources. My advice is to try to focus on regenerating energy, not only from people, from spending time with our loved ones, buried in our friends and family all the time, but also to give importance to those timeless resources.

When we fall into this world, we are allocated with a certain amount of time. Some have a larger portion of time, while others have a more modest appearance on earth. The point is that each one of us is running out of time every day; therefore, we need to be aware of this fact and use our time wisely. I don't mean that we have to be on the go, breathless from all the things we want to get done, but even starting and ending by recognizing this simple, obvious fact is

---

[5] "Miles Davis (1926 – 1991) - an American jazz trumpeter, bandleader, and composer" (Biography)

a huge progression for our human species that has a genuine lunatic nature. The average life expectancy in the world is about seventy-one years, and this is one of the best-case scenarios. We don't necessarily operate in a bundle together with our loved ones.

Life is full of encounters, separations, births, and deaths. It's a full cycle and product line with emotional roller costars, and we will struggle if we attach ourselves fully and solely to others because people are not timeless.

I suggest that you pick your preferred resource: are you more of a beach bum or a ski bunny? Or maybe you are a jungle enthusiast. Why not? Mariya likes beaches, being born and raised by the sea, leaving a blueprint I can't ignore. In London, Paris, Saõ Paulo, Toluca, or you name it, I always looked for the sea, the ocean, or any big body of water.

Maybe you have a special relationship with your camera or perhaps the mountains, and that's also a great source. What matters is to identify how to deliberately manipulate yourself to keep the right balance at all times and direct your mind, body, and soul toward the upper levels of your potential. Keep your friends close, love your family, and be there for them, but learn when and how to detach yourself in order to take the path toward a personal evolution, outside of your comfort zone, and sometimes this is away from your roots. Stay anchored in your mind, not physically rooted to one spot, and time will do the rest for you!

The Structure behind the Shiny Vitrine

Chapter 7. Plan of Action: University Exchange Programs

A goal without a plan is just a wish.

—Antoine de Saint-Exupéry[6]

Part I

List of Acronyms: University Years

- First-Year License 1 (L1): First Year of Bachelor's Degree

- Second-Year License 2 (L2): Second Year of Bachelor's Degree

- Third-Year License 3 (L3): Third and Last Year of Bachelor's Degree

- Fourth-Year Master 1 (M1): Master's Degree I

- Fifth-Year Master 2 (M2): Master's Degree II

- Semester: "In colleges and universities in some countries, a semester is one of the two main periods into which the year is divided" (Collins English dictionary).

- Exchange Program: "An arrangement in which people from different countries visit each other's country, perhaps to strengthen links between them or to improve foreign language skills" (Collins English dictionary).

First-Year License 1 (L1): First Year of Bachelor's Degree

Focus on your studies and finding a stable part-time job, make new friends, and do your best to validate your first year at the university. When you enroll at school and have to select your non-mandatory classes in terms of choice (not in terms of credits from those classes mandatory to have), think carefully before choosing a language class you resonate with. This moment will play a major role in your exchange program project. The language you select will represent one of the pillars you will need in the next stage of your multi-layered project.

Yes, you must start building it as of now. Choose the right language now; otherwise the system might block you later. Try to stick to the same language you select every year throughout your entire university path for consistency reasons. It will have a very positive impact later if you do this.

---

[6] "Antoine de Saint-Exupéry (1900 – 1944) - a French writer, poet, aristocrat, journalist and pioneering aviator, wrote the 'Little Prince'" (Biography)

I chose Portuguese and Spanish. I hardly learned anything in either one of the classes. The university was on strike during that period, but the fact I had participated in such an activity gave me credibility in front of the decision-makers and signature providers as proof from my faculty that I would manage to be educated in Portuguese first and later in Spanish. I had to reassure them on two separate occasions in the exchange program preparations for Brazil in L3 and then for Mexico in M1 that I would be able to navigate in the host countries, I would not fail to complete my semesters abroad, there would not be room for failure, and I would represent the university with pride.

Second-Year License 2 (L2): Second Year of Bachelor's Degree

Focus on your regular studies and your part-time job. Enjoy the time with friends and start preparing your international university exchange program, which should ideally take place in L3. Start preparing the process early, during the first semester of L2. No, it is not too early. This is exactly the right time. Don't miss those deadlines!

Go to the secretariat of your faculty. The experience of visiting this office may relate to the scene from the secretariat, filmed in the mythical and also very inspiring Franco-Spanish movie that took place in Barcelona, following the steps of a French exchange student. The film is called *Spanish Hostel,* or *Auberge espagnole* in French. This is where I got the idea to embark on exchange programs! Playful mind, right?

Go to the international relations department any university or institution has in some form and ask where you should look for concrete information on the exchange programs depending on your discipline. They will guide you further.

Go on the website of your university and find the section dedicated to the university exchange programs offered by the organization. Research which programs are linked to it and are relevant for your major. During this year, try to investigate both:

- Option 1: exchange program of one year abroad … or ideally

- Option 2: exchange program of one semester abroad

If you opt for option 2, you should select to complete this during the second semester. I will explain why you should select this rather than focus on a year abroad. Also it is better to go for the second semester to go abroad.

Now as you are doing the research on available and suitable exchange programs for L3 anyway, try to investigate your potential options for an exchange program in M1 too.

Remember, try to anticipate your actions and choices. If you do the research exercise simultaneously while you are doing your personal investigation for the future exchange program in L3, you will gain time and be able to start building the third layer of your project planned for M1. Technically, you are preparing yourself to study abroad twice before you've even left for the first time. (Refer to chapter 4.) This is another trick most students fail to detect and then miss opportunities!

Yes, you need to anticipate ways in advance the actions you want to take, think through every move you make, and develop a great awareness of time. Remember, chapter 6 dedicated to the notion of time. Well, you can do the math. Can you?

Compile all the information and documents and submit it to the international relations department before the deadlines. I have prepared an example of documents that the university may potentially require. Each program and university (home and host) has its own specific set of documents. The below mock-up is an example for your reference, to provide you with additional guidance and reassurance. Usually all documents must be provided in the language of the home country and translated in the relevant language of the host university/country. For instance, my two set of documents were prepared in French and Portuguese for the exchange program in L3, which I chose for the showcase below.

- Curriculum Vitae (CV)

- Cover letter (CL)

I made the CV/résumé and wrote the cover letter in French myself. I didn't know any Lusophone-speaking people who could help me. I was about to get blocked at this stage when I got the idea that the university has all kinds of intellectual and cultural resources.

So to provide myself with such a letter in Portuguese, I kindly knocked on the door of an unknown Brazilian teacher from the Lusophone faculty and asked politely for some help with my project. You can use a similar source for this exercise if you encounter difficulties. To access the letter that I used (and know works), please click here or go to matg.co.uk Also include the following:

- A recommendation letter from a teacher from the home university

  ○ I asked my own teacher from the Portuguese classes I had enrolled in the previous year.

- A statement showing your grades for the accomplished year(s) and semester(s)

- University enrollment certificate, to be issued by the home university

  ○ You'll most likely be able to download it from your university personal profile account.

- Application form provided from your home university in which you state your choices of disciplines and universities you are interested in studying at on an exchange basis

- The director of your discipline commonly discusses, signs, and stamps this form. You need to present and explain your project to the person in charge of your major, stating clearly why you want to study in this respective university and country, what you want to learn from the exchange program, and so forth.

- Copy of your passport

- The application form provided from the host university

  - This form will have the look and feel of the foreign university documents and will be in the respective language.

- Identity photo

- Health insurance

- Letter (proof of level of knowledge of the respective foreign language)

  - For the provision of such a letter, you will need to liaise with your respective non-mandatory language class teacher(s) from the previous year(s) and kindly ask to support you in your project by writing such a statement for you. In the statement, the teacher should include that you attended their language class, (e.g., Portuguese) the previous year and had satisfying grades, you are willing to learn more, and you now need exposure to the respective language, and culture. To access the letter I used (and know works), please click here or go to matg.co.uk

Prepare envelopes in an A4/letter format and stamps to be sent out with the whole application file. On the front of the envelopes, you will most likely have to pre-write the name, address, faculty, and name of the contact person at the international relations department receiving you at the host university. This must be ready to ensure you are not an administrative burden for the host university.

I strongly recommend submitting applications for at least three countries with a minimum of three universities per country, if the home university of course allows. You need to aim high and broad. Remember the trick from "Mise en Abyme," the preparation to study in, for instance, France, and chapter 4.

You have done a great job so far. You want to do an exchange program. Then prepare yourself that your first choice may not be accepted; therefore you need to target several locations that appeal to you and where you can anticipate spending a good six months of your life there.

Third-Year License 3 (L3): Third and Last Year of Bachelor's Degree

Focus on your regular studies and part-time job. Enjoy the time with your friends and start preparing your second international university exchange program, which should ideally take place in M1.

Before you leave for the university exchange program taking place, ideally in the second semester of L3, apply the same approach as you did in L2, described previously for your convenience.

As advised, you should by now have a good idea of where you would like to go again before even leaving for your first exchange program. Now in the first semester of L3 (that's why you need to be on-site and hands-on) is the time to submit the application files for your second university exchange program before you have embarked on the first one. Read "Mise en Abyme" of layer 2 in chapter 4.

Yes, this is correct, you need to plan these things way in advance if you want to parachute twice in a row and land on the target each time. I cannot repeat it enough: don't miss those deadlines!

Go back to the secretariat of your faculty to ask for information. This time it will be easier since you should know the path already. Go to the international relations department of your university or similar institution and ask where you should look for information relating to your discipline. Inform them that you are about to go on an exchange program in the next semester. This would automatically mean that you no longer have priority in the choices of universities you make if all available spots are full because students who apply for the first time have the priority overall (like you the first time).

In practical terms, it is better to play a low profile and select less popular universities. You need to target universities that tend to have open spots. If you get accepted to do an exchange program twice in a row, the second time you lose your priority. Your acceptance the second time should be perceived as a bonus and treated as such. Go to your university's website and find the section dedicated to the exchange programs they offer. You should be familiar with the pattern by now.

During this year, try to investigate possibilities for an exchange program, ideally for one semester abroad, and this semester should be for the second semester. I will explain why you should focus on the second semester again.

In order to be able to reset and organize yourself properly in between exchange programs, you will need quality time without stressing yourself out but rather making sure the project is going smoothly. It is better, in my opinion, to do a semester abroad in two different countries and ideally aim for perfection in two foreign languages than only one either way. If you opt for a year abroad, it requires heavier preparation, but it is entirely up to you to organize this part of the project.

Compile the information, for example, requested forms and recommendation and cover letters. Translate your grades and submit your file in order to apply again for at least three countries with a minimum of three universities per country. You need to aim high and broad, high meaning reaching the moon (your target) and broad meaning reaching for the stars, which is the equivalent of the "next best thing." Sometimes, the "next best thing" is the best thing.

To access the letter, I used (and know works), please click here or go to matg.co.uk I am not including the example of a list of documents, as it will most likely be similar to the one I introduced you to above in L2, ahead of the preparations for L3. In any event, the concept remains the same, and this is what you should be tapping into.

You have done a great job so far. You want to study abroad, so prepare yourself that you might not be accepted with your first choice. Therefore you need to target several locations that all resonate with you in some way.

Part II

Education is our passport to the future. Tomorrow belongs to people, who prepare for it today.

—Malcolm X[7]

Fourth-Year Master 1 (M1): Master's Degree I

Upon your return from the semester abroad in L3, take a deep breath, focus on your part-time student job, and enjoy the time with your friends. In Master 1 (M1), you need to decide if you should stay and continue to study in M2 in the same discipline at the same university or if you would like to change and apply elsewhere. I chose the latter.

If you decide to change university/discipline in M2, you need to do your university research now in the first semester of M1 or prepare the applications while you are abroad on your exchange program. Then send the applications to France out of the country you are located in at this moment. If you followed the guidelines, you should be studying abroad at the stage of the application process and have admissions on file for M2. I applied at seven universities to do my Master 2 (M2): six in Lyon and one in Paris. I was accepted at the Sorbonne University in Paris, so I embarked on this new adventure.

Fifth-Year Master 2 (M2): Master's Degree II

In Master 2 (M2), you will need to focus on internships and kick-start your professional career. In the section dedicated to my internship program in the United States in Chicago, I share my position and opinion about the internships versus the university exchange programs. If you wish to learn how and why you should prioritize exchange programs over internships, I invite you to read the episode about Chicago.

Here, depending on how you evaluate and relate to the proposed guidelines, story, phases, adventures, and challenges illustrated in the action plan, as well as the concrete episodes I have put together for you, do not worry if the read does not resonate with you. This does not mean that you are on the wrong track; it just means that it is not your track.

Even though the plan of action might look complex or overwhelming, trust me, it's a very down-to-earth process with a happy ending. Once you join the structure in the name of the university, everything will go with the flow, as I describe in my stories in the next episodes from around the globe.

---

[7] "Malcolm X (1925 – 1965) - an African American Muslim minister and human rights activist" (Biography)

The Structure behind the Shiny Vitrine

Chapter 8. Scholarships and a Compilation of Other Resources

Study hard what interests you the most in the most undisciplined, irrelevant and original manner possible.

—Richard Feynmann[8]

Here are two scenarios showcasing financial engines that can help you realize your dream project.

1. French State Help: Studying in France Only

Update of the information 2020/2021

Type of Resource

"CROUS Bourse sur des critères sociaux," or a low family-income scholarship, is available for any French and/or EU/EEA/Switzerland students with low family income.

Benefits

- It varies from €1,020 ($1,117) to € 5,612 ($6,693) per year, depending on your parental income.

- Check on the website above what proof of documents you need to provide exactly.

- The lower your parental income is, the higher the scholarship is. The scholarship is equally distributed and transferred each month directly to your account based on a minimum ten and maximum twelve months basis per year, depending on your situation.

- The university tuition fees and health insurance are free of charge under this scholarship. You pay the administrative costs only, which are more than symbolic.

- You don't need to pay the student campus life contribution, which would cost you another €91 ($100), if you don't have this scholarship.

- It gives you priority in the university housing allocation.

Type of Resource

La CAF, "Allocations familiales," is monthly financial state help with the rent.

---

[8] "Richard Feynmann (1918 – 1988) - an African American Muslim minister and human rights activist" (Biography)

Benefit

- The help is allocated based on primarily your yearly income, the price of your rent, if it is a shared flat or not, the number of people sharing the flat, their unique and combined income, the surface you occupy, and the flat's location. The amount you will be allocated will be distributed and transferred each month directly to your bank account.

Type of Resource

La PUMA (ex-CMU, "Couverture maladie universelle") is state health insurance for people with low income.

Benefits

- All your health-related expenses are covered 100 percent.

- The public transport pass costs only €18,20 ($20) per month if you have it.

- Check the Public Transport site.

2. **French State Help Compilation: Exchange Program Abroad**

Update of the information 2020/2021

Type of Resource

"CROUS Bourse sur des critères sociaux," or a low family-income scholarship, is available for any French and/or EU/EEA/Switzerland students with low family income.

Benefits

- It varies from €1,020 ($1,117) to €5,612 ($6,693) per year, depending on your parental income.

- Check on the website above what proof of documents you need to provide exactly.

- The lower your parental income is, the higher the scholarship is. The scholarship is equally distributed and transferred each month directly to your account, on a minimum ten and maximum twelve months basis per year, depending on your situation.

- The university tuition fees and health insurance are free of charge under this scholarship. You pay the administrative costs only, which are more than symbolic.

- You don't need to pay the student campus life contribution, which would cost you another €91 ($100), if you don't have this scholarship.

- It gives you priority in the university housing allocation.

Type of Resource

La CAF, **"Allocations familiales,"** is monthly financial state help with the rent.

Benefit

- The financial help is allocated based primarily on your yearly income, the price of your rent, if it is a shared flat or not, the number of people sharing the flat, their unique and combined income, the surface you occupy, and the flat's location. The amount you will be allocated will be distributed and transferred each month directly to your bank account.

Type of Resource

La PUMA (ex-CMU, "Couverture maladie universelle) is health insurance state help for people with low income.

Benefits

- All your health-related expenses are covered 100 percent.

- The public transport pass costs only €18, 20 ($20) per month, if you have CMU.

- Check the Public Transport site.

3. **French State Help: Exchange Program Abroad**

Update of the information 2020/2021

Type of Resource

"CROUS Bourse sur des critères sociaux," or a low family-income scholarship, is available for any French and/or EU/EEA/Switzerland students with low family income.

Benefits

- It varies from €1,020 ($1,117) to €5,612 ($6,693) per year depending on your parental income.

- The lower the parental income the higher the scholarship is. The state help is equally distributed and transferred each month directly to your bank account based on a minimum ten and maximum twelve months per year, depending on your situation.

Type of Resource

"Bourse de mobilité internationale sur des critères sociaux," or a low family-income scholarship, is available for any French and/or EU/EEA/Switzerland students with low family income that have qualified to go to an exchange program to study abroad.

Benefits

- This scholarship is cumulative. That is, the student would receive it in conjunction with the same scholarship they would naturally receive if staying in France. This scholarship is an extension, like a bonus, in addition to the first one, if you have qualified, of course, for the exchange program. Both scholarships are not self-exclusive, but cumulative. This applies only if you qualify for the above scholarship given for parental low income.

- The monthly payments could be around €400 ($438) and are given from minimum of two to nine months maximum, depending on the amount of time spent abroad.

Type of Resource

"Bourse régionale de mobilité internationale" is a regional exchange program scholarship in, for example, Auvergne-Rhône-Alpes.

Benefits

- The scholarship is eligible for the respective region. In the Auvergne-Rhône-Alpes, for example, if you study in a public university in this region, you can benefit from around additional €95 ($105) per week during your exchange program, which are given for a minimum of four and a maximum of twenty-six weeks.

- In addition, another state help could be allocated, but only if you already qualify for the low-income scholarship, which varies from around €80 ($88) to €530 ($580), depending on your income situation and how low it is. This package is a one-shot additional help from your region, usually transferred to your bank account as soon as you arrive at the destination.

I would like to let you do the breakdown of benefits, if you enter in the criteria for low-income student exchange program scholarships deployed by the state of France via Crous and the relevant regional body.

NB!

I can give you the links to a myriad of financial resources and provide you with this compilation of compliable scholarships, but the truth is that if you don't resonate with the mindset, concept, and philosophy illustrated in the parts The Structure behind the Shiny Vitrine, As Above So Below, and Mise en Abyme, you will never make use of the above-mentioned links and financial resources.

Practical Knowledge

Chapter 9. How to Juggle Student Life and a Job

There is no substitute for hard work.

—Thomas A. Edison[9]

As I already mentioned during my time at university in Lyon, I worked as a bartender at a popular Irish bar I was introduced to by an ex-boyfriend of mine, who shortly after left my life. This hidden gem in the old part of town, where everybody knows your name, offered a complete immersion into the Anglo-Saxon English-speaking world. While working there, I felt like I was living in two completely different countries simultaneously, like experiencing a dual reality effect, overlapping on the same timeline.

What mattered was that I was earning money and my English was improving by the day. My performance at school also improved, ironically thanks to work, as I was benefitting from my new English-speaking world I had found in France. I used my newly gained linguistic skills wisely. I applied it to improve my school performance and to see a clearer purpose in this journey of mine. Additionally I had moved in with friends to live above the bar. Refer to chapter 10 if you want to learn more about the accommodation situation.

The financially stable and friendly structure I needed was finally established. The working hours at the bar correlated to my school timetable, so that both activities didn't overlap. I had a cozy home and a carefully-thought-out ecosystem that I had created to sustain myself. This ecosystem provided me with regular cash flow and access to food and alcohol at preferential rates thanks to my job and my apartment as well as time saved from the microscopic commute to work, all important ingredients for every student. My job also helped me establish stable friendships via the network I had built of interesting and inspiring English-speaking customers and colleagues.

This university of life represented my biggest comfort zone for many years. I cherished every day I was surrounded by so many friendly, generous, wise people and life mentors. I was benefitting from their presence in my life. I let them guide and teach me on my way to a higher reality. During these fragile student years, I felt privileged to be spending time with such special individuals, moreover in the context of work.

While I was bartending in Lyon, I kept making useful connections by naturally befriending more and more sympathetic people through work. I believed there was a purpose I was letting selected figures enter my life. These people were going to play a role in it at some stage. I

---

[9] "Thomas A. Edison (1847 – 1931) - an American inventor and businessman who has been described as America's greatest inventor" (Biography)

trusted my intuition that some of these seemingly random people I kept meeting were keepers. They often represented a source of inspiration, knowledge, and wisdom. I could learn from the conversation in the downtime during a random shift, if I were able to focus on chitchatting while serving beer all the better, to filter their useful stories and information. When I was not working or studying, we simply partied together, and the regulars became my true friends.

Job Insights and Practical Information

Full-time employment in France is thirty-five hours per week. Hereafter, you may consult the minimum wage table I have prepared for your reference.

Minimum Wage

Wage	Gross	Net
Hourly	€10,15 ($12)	€8,03 ($9,6)
Daily	€71,05 ($85)	€56.21 ($67,1)
Monthly (35h)	€ 1539.42 ($1,838)	€1217,91 ($1,453,83)

Source (Service Public 2020)

NB!

Advice: do not work more than twenty-five hours a week since you must study. Remember your purpose!

Your target is to work between twenty hours minimum and twenty-five hours maximum per week. My advice is to secure twenty hours of part-time work at one or even two student jobs in order to be comfortable financially. Having secured this stable income, you should live comfortably in combination with the scholarships. Read chapter 8. This financially resourceful structure will establish a soil with favorable conditions, allowing you to dedicate the rest of your quality time to studying or rather learning. I intentionally use the word "quality time" because you should actually rely on your leftover time to produce decent homework, deliver quality research, and validate your years at school. It will work, believe me.

Be careful not to go over the limit of twenty-five hours per week I identified as the limit, trust me. Without maintaining the right balance, you might put your education at risk and your future in jeopardy for the wrong reasons. Remember, at this stage of your life, you haven't yet started to build your professional career; therefore don't get distracted by momentums that you may come across as your priority is to graduate (bachelor's degree) and ideally move to post-graduate (master's degree), all in one seamless flow.

Don't postpone your studies. Get it done and out of the way. Tick the box and you will never regret it!

Examples of Student Part-Time Jobs

Babysitting, housekeeping, moving furniture, waitressing, or any type of hospitality work fits, and my favorite was bartending in an Irish pub. Why bartending? Well, this *métier*, or profession, is special. It is going to teach you many hidden yet transferable skills that you can use later in life in the corporate world that people underestimate tremendously. The following multitude of wonderful transferable skills that you can learn are applicable in any type of professional environment.

Transferable Skills Bartender to Corporate World

A bartender is a good listener. It exposes you to all kinds of conversations, some interesting and some not so. It accustoms you to work under pressure. It allows you to practice English and naturally master it. You will gain exposure to a myriad of English accents (e.g., American, Australian, Canadian, English, Irish, Northern Irish, Scottish, South African, Walsh, etc.) with which you will have to deal with in a fast-paced environment.

You may even save money from eating lunch and/or dinner if the place serves food. Ideally you should organize yourself to be scheduled to work during the lunch shifts and on weekends, taking night shifts occasionally.

Bartending teaches you to watch out that no one gets drunk and builds your confidence. It develops your emotional intelligence to get quick information about the customers you are dealing with, develops your friendliness, intuition and customer awareness, and verbal communication skills.

It enhances your social skills. It's a great place to learn about many different cultures and builds up your general culture knowledge and openness to the world. It teaches you initiative, motivation, proactivity, and integrity. It will teach you to take it easy on the shots (alcohol awareness) but increases your selling ability by making sure the customers come, stay longer, and return.

It makes you easily approachable by people who barely know you and increases persuasiveness. You can pitch or elevate discussions with customers. It also teaches resistance, staff and crowd management, adaptation, flexibility, and how to build a network and make people feel at ease with you.

You learn teamwork and the ability to be a team player. The bartender has a mixture of roles: artist, accountant, housekeeper, police officer, psychiatrist, interior designer, sergeant major, and mother all rolled into one. The bartender is balancing a host of elements in his mind, which teaches you how to juggle with situations simultaneously. The bartender makes sure the atmosphere is nice, plays the right music at the right time, and sets the tone for everything that happens in the bar.

It teaches you time and management prioritization. When you work for tips, you work harder and better to get better tips, for example, commission-based corporate jobs. You become a storyteller, which is a great skill for presentations. You will develop skills to make customers willing to stay and talk to you and simultaneously spend money. You will naturally learn how to engage people and maintain conversation. You would naturally become comfortable in a sales-oriented environment.

Bartending in an English-speaking bar is my best student career advice and is to be considered if you get bored of the corporate world too. You will get bored from it quicker than you think, trust me.

Practical Knowledge

Chapter 10. Accommodations, Food, and Other Expenses

You don't need a silver fork to eat good food.

—Paul Prudhomme[10]

Accommodations

My favorite TV show of all time is *Friends*. I was perhaps a little inspired by these fictional characters and Rachel Green. I moved into a charming and typical old town-style apartment in Lyon, upstairs from the bar where I worked (the equivalent of the Central Perk in *Friends*). I moved in together with two girlfriends and lived happily on this bustling Lyonnaise street for several years.

Price and Location

The prices of the flats vary depending on the location and surface (measured in square meters) of course. I am positive that with a bit of luck and a good dose of thorough research, you can find a convenient flat for the price of less than a €1000 ($1,095) per month in a relatively central location in a city outside of a Paris-type megapolis.

Guarantors

The tricky part in renting a flat in France is that you need a guarantor, a tough step you cannot avoid in France. Don't worry about it because I have a solution for you. You can contact a service called Loca-Pass that can help you overcome the "*caution*" or the guarantee of your future shared flat-to-be. This specific service put in place in France can help you with this task (unless you have friends that can help you with).

Food and Going Out

My best advice is to learn and accustom yourself to cooking at home, to learn tasty recipes. Most likely, preparing all kinds of tasty pasta recipes is going to be part of your weekly menu.

Other Examples:

- Price of baguette: as of €0,90 ($1)

- A bottle of great local French wine: as of €3,4 ($3,7)

- Meat: affordable prices

---

[10] "Paul Prudhomme (1940 – 2015) - an American celebrity chef" (Biography)

- Vegetables: from the weekend markets, purchase a big quantity of vegetables at a decent price (avoid the supermarkets)

- Restaurant lunch and dinner menus: France is the home of some of the most phenomenal restaurants worldwide. The prices of the menus in the down to earth restaurants are more than affordable. Eating in a restaurant is part of the French lifestyle. The moment you become part of the culture, even as a student, you won't be deprived from such experiences on regular basis.

Entertainment Costs

- Cinema ticket student price: about €8 ($8,7), depending on the movie theatres

- Café theatre, opera, and concerts: with your student status, you will be able to attend all kinds of cultural events either completely free or at a symbolic cost when you show your student ID card. This is your best ticket to culture at the age between eighteen and twenty-five. Use it wisely and with abundance. France is the mecca of all kinds of cultural events; therefore no student at this age range will be deprived access to culture and learning.

- Museums: free entry usually for students under the age of twenty-six by showing a student ID

Traveling

SNCF, the high-speed train network, also offers preferential prices and fidelity cards for students under the age of twenty-six. If you have a low-income scholarship, you could benefit from additional discounts. I am not providing you with the website because there are several ways and paths to student discounts, if you wish to travel. I will let you do the research yourself and tailor the answers to meet your needs.

From Around the Globe

Episode: Brazil and South America, Exchange Program

In my heart I never left Brazil.

—Brent Spiner[11]

Now let's see what the outcome was of the plan of action I shared with you earlier and check its credibility.

My journeys at the university in Lyon were scattered. The mandatory classes I chose were based on the available slots outside of my work schedule, and the classes were not necessarily my preferences. The truth is, I couldn't afford to enroll in every available subject in the major I wanted to learn about since I had an unapologetic desire for knowledge of all kinds. I had to work to pay the living costs and the bills. I had to take care of myself, so I didn't have much spare time for extravagant subjects, I had to start my learning from scratch. I was aware though that I was skilled with languages, naturally curious, and at least in this field I had a higher performance than the rest of the crowd in general. I had identified that in these circumstances, my ability to learn languages effortlessly was going to be my strategy to validate my bachelor's degree. Incidentally, this approach also helped me protect my laziness regarding other not-so-appealing subjects, where it was required to focus and study slightly harder.

---

[11] "Brent Spiner (1949) - is an American actor, comedian, musician and singer, who played in Star Trek" (Biography)

France is well known for its culture and infatuation with striking in order to solve a problem. The approach in my university was no different. During my first semester in L2, I had enrolled in a Portuguese class for beginners. I only participated in a few sessions. In one of which, the professor distributed a piece of paper asking students to sign it in case anyone was interested to go on an exchange program to Brazil. What do you think? Did I sign it? Of course I did! Then I forgot about this seemingly insignificant action and carelessly archived it away in my mind. I never returned to this class, as the university then went on strike. The first semester of L2 was over.

I had failed. I failed both the exchange program to the United States I had applied for and my semester. I failed to go to Tulane University in New Orleans, even though I'd successfully passed the TOEFEL exam and the host university had accepted me.

This failed semester in Lyon blocked my US project. I had not channeled my energy correctly. I had let myself go. I was too busy having fun at work in the bar and misused my time hanging out with my new exciting entourage. I got distracted and messed up my priorities. I was deeply upset from my weak performance and the giant fiasco I had created for myself. I had learned my lesson the hard way. What do you expect? Simply Mariya!

My performance had not thrilled me. I was not living up to my potential, and it was staring me in the face. I realized that I needed to focus in order to compensate for my first semester and take advantage of the second chance I had been given to validate my year at the very least. At that moment, I wasn't aware that the validation of the school year was my ticket to Brazil. Nonetheless, I lacked motivation. I was not focused and was missing the spark in me.

One random day of this incredible, nonlinear life, I received an email of acknowledgement of my application, informing me that I had been accepted to apply to study at the University of São Paulo, Brazil, for one semester via the university foreign exchange program. Bam! My motivation was back on track. I validated my year and prepared to embark on this new adventure. I informed all my friends, colleagues, and, most importantly, my managers at the bar that I was about to be absent for a few months because Mariya was going to drink caipirinha (Brazilian mojito-type drink) on the beach in São Paulo. I believed that this was my true purpose after winning a ticket to be part of this adventure following my signature on a random piece of paper in the Portuguese class for beginners.

However, after double-checking the details, I realized that I still had to go through the whole application process, as described in chapters 7 and 8. Nonetheless, the carrot was in front of me, and I did everything I could to obtain it!

I must be honest with you: at that point, I had no significant intention to study once I made it to Brazil. I was not particularly passionate about learning Portuguese either. My sole purpose was to travel, and if this were feasible via the exchange program, I was more than happy to try. I was not at all familiar with São Paulo and believed it to be located near the south coast, and I immediately envisaged the exotic coastal lifestyle.

When the time came, I gathered my friends and colleagues together for a farewell party, and the following day, I headed to São Paulo very casually, as if I were going on a trip to London. Conveniently or coincidently, I had met a lovely Brazilian couple in Lyon a few months prior to my trip. They offered to host me for the beginning of my stay.

Luckily the universe knew better than me because upon arrival, I quickly realized that São Paulo was not on the beach. Back at the time, we had no reflex to ask Uncle Google about every question we may have. So, upon arrival I realized that São Paulo was a concrete jungle covered in skyscrapers with helicopters overhead because it has amongst the heaviest traffic jams in the world. Back then, late 2000's, the city was rated number three amongst the most dangerous cities in the world, and the *favelas* (shanty towns) were to be avoided.

I did not know how to navigate this megapolis, let alone avoid the *favelas*. I was not only confused about how I was going to survive, I was terrified from the fact that I could not understand a word of what anyone was saying. I couldn't understand Portuguese. Nobody spoke English, and if someone out there hadn't laid the bed for me by introducing me to the young Brazilian couple back in Lyon prior to the adventure, I swear I had no survival plan. The family I stayed with spoke English, which was comforting. However, the lovely housekeeper was particularly intrigued to have a foreigner in the house. She desperately wanted to share her knowledge about the Brazilian culture with me and wanted to benefit from the fact that I came from a foreign land. The lady had questions! Her curiosity and determination to communicate pushed me to construct and communicate my first phrases in Portuguese the following week.

My life in Brazil started smoothly. Or so I thought. Two weeks after my arrival in Brazil, the university finally opened after the summer break, which takes place in December and January (Southern Hemisphere), and I went to enroll in my classes. I was told I needed a student visa; otherwise I couldn't enroll in any of the classes and in any event couldn't stay longer than three months in the country. Hmmm, Mariya faced a project-threatening situation that I had to take care of ASAP (as soon as possible).

I made a little detour and flew back to Paris the following day as soon as I realized what I needed to do. Applying for a student visa out of Paris was not an issue; the visa would be granted. The issue stemmed from reading a random resource that conveniently stated that it was possible to apply for a student visa once you are in the host country. From today's perspective, it makes absolutely no sense, but back then, the solution seemed convenient. It was unrealistic but convenient.

Why did I believe this information without double-checking it? Because I was tired from juggling university and work and was counting the days to make it to Brazil. I wanted to be able to focus and then do the visa, so this information was welcomed. Wrong, darling. After two weeks of paperwork, enjoying Paris while the visa was organized (luckily I had my friends who hosted me), and having €800 ($877) later, Mariya was on the road again, heading back to Brazil, now all set with a fresh new student visa and armed with a lifelong lesson.

My life in Brazil started smoothly for a second time. São Paulo's diversity, multitude of ethnicities, and mix of features on people's faces mesmerized me. The city was a true melting pot, from Italian (Bixiga) to Lebanese neighborhoods and the Japanese quarter (Liberdade). I could get lost every day in a new country if I wanted to because the city offered it.

My time in Brazil and the fact I learned to speak Portuguese fluently left a blueprint on my entire life afterwards. The experiences I gained there, the exposure to this exotic culture full of mysticism, shaped my life ahead. I fell sick with chicken pox and got robbed in Salvador's Pelourinho by a seven-year-old *moleque* (street kid in Portuguese) with a machete in his hand. I almost got bitten by a venomous snake in the Pantanal swamp and swam with piranhas in the muddy rivers next to the Bolivian borders in the state of Campo Grande. I experienced a whole range of adventures, and I strongly recommend this open-minded approach.

Go out there and meet new cultures and learn languages. It gives you a completely new attitude toward how you see yourself and the way you filter information about the world. It changes your perceptions and tastes, helps broaden your knowledge, and makes you more aware. Maybe my readers are fascinated by Japan and resonate better with Asian cultures and languages. My advice is to go for it and explore.

Throughout my stay in Brazil, I had to study hard, catch up with the language, and start understanding my new environment. It was crucial because I'd arrived with a tourist's mindset, with no basis of Portuguese, and it did not do me any favors. Luckily I managed to channel my energy and focus. I started understanding the pattern of this new exotic language with the speed of lightning. Brazil was a special, intriguing place, charged with a lot of unfamiliar energy, and I responded to a new rainbow of frequencies in terms of infrastructure, social behavior, and values combined. I wanted to explore its every corner and take full advantage of this random adventure I had organized for myself. My alert system was on, always blinking red, behind the euphoric state of my naïve inner world and the feeling of being privileged to be present in this new land. It raised my awareness regarding one major issue: Brazil was a dangerous place. My first words in Portuguese were not something silly, as it is usually the case, but "Escuro, Cuidado, Perigoso" ("Dark, Careful, Danger").

I knew immediately that I couldn't afford to misjudge or underestimate a situation again, regardless of its scale, as I could be doomed for real next time. The feeling of insecurity pushed my senses open and triggered access to unsuspected knowledge fed from another dimension with the intention to protect me via my own awareness. I had one purpose, to travel as much as my eyes, heart, and soul could bear and of course as much as my student scholarship wallet could afford, it being the primary determinate.

I made good friends with the rest of the 'lost' foreign exchange students who had discovered and implemented the same plan of action as me, which brought us together. No wonder why we got along so well in no time, as a Greek proverb says, "Great minds think alike." We travelled together from Salvador de Bahia to the swamps in Pantanal. We passed by Force d'Iguaçu's Waterfalls National Park and visited Buenos Aires (Argentina) and Montevideo (Uruguay).

Speaking of Argentina, this is where I had my first encounter with Hispanic-speaking South America. I was unhappy I could not communicate with the locals as not everyone could understand my Portugnol (a pigeon language mixture between Portuguese and Spanish), and English was no longer of use in these distant lands.

Ah! A new idea was born. I needed to learn to speak Spanish as soon as possible. It was mandatory. A new inspiring goal was set. Now it was a matter of when and where this goal was going to be accomplished and for it to become a reality. My mind was on its way to design another new pattern with the aim to get myself into another similar context. I had to focus, stay alert for future opportunities, and target the next destination more carefully (this time), one that would accommodate Mariya's adventurous spirit.

I am not going to bore you with the description of the beautiful landscapes of Brazil's jungles, beaches, and marshlands that I had the privilege to see with my own eyes as I will let you discover this part on my Instagram account at *mariya_atg*.

From Around the Globe

Episode: Chicago (USA), Summer Internship

I miss everything about Chicago, except January and February.

—Gary Cole[12]

There was more on that plan of action. Let's see what next adventure is hosted in this episode.

After I returned from Brazil, I was back in the swing of it, back to university in Lyon and back to working at the bar I had left more than six months earlier. Everything was working more or less smoothly; however as you may guess, there was one small issue. I learned the sad news that I had failed to validate my third year of my bachelor's degree due to an administrative mistake. I had no means to prove or fix anything at that late stage because when the issue was still fixable, I was somewhere in South America, and trust me, it was worth it.

I was forced to cope with this fact I had failed a semester, resulting in having to take the whole school year again at the end of the day. I tried to look on the bright side because my mind was gifted enough to find a positive side in every situation without discouraging myself or letting myself go.

I motivated myself to retake the failed semester, which left me with half a school year free. It was the perfect time to unleash my creativity and force my genius to fabricate a brilliant new plan in order to channel my energy and occupy myself in a constructive way.

---

[12] "Gary Cole (1956) - an American actor and voice actor" (Biography)

I was brutally honest with myself. Yes, I was super happy serving beer at the bar and acting as if I were a character in the film *Coyote Ugly*. I had invaluable exposure to a diverse range of the English language, thanks to my job. In addition, my English flatmate and my English-speaking boyfriend had given me stable knowledge about the language, as well as firsthand references about the Anglo-Saxon culture. My English was getting stronger by the day, and I already had four fluent languages under my belt; however—yes, again, however—something was missing.

I mentioned to friends and customers that I was entertaining the idea of doing a professional internship. One of the bar customers was enthusiastic in helping Mariya's cause. This customer, a highly positioned charismatic and magnetic expat, arranged an interview for me the following week. I failed the interview, but this failure taught me three important things:

1. Never underestimate the importance of your entourage and always be happy to network.

2. I had zero corporate experience, which exposed a new obstacle I had to overcome.

3. I had no certified (yet) or professional explanation as to why I spoke fluent English, and I needed an alibi for the outside world to justify where I obtained this language and, more importantly, how I had come to master it because clearly this hard skill was not formed at the university solely.

These conventional thinking decision-makers that saturate the corporate world did not or would not accept the fact that I had become fluent in English through my job at a local Irish bar in a French city. My inner world and close friends knew my abilities to incorporate information. Thanks to my sharp memory the language stuck in my memory without any effort, I was clearly aware of this function of my mind, and I took advantage of it. That's why it was there, to be exploited. It was mine to do so. But who cared about my small little world, right? I needed an alibi.

I had to postpone the Spanish project in order to get myself to an English-speaking country as soon as possible. Now was the time to focus and get access to the content in my head, leading me as usual to a new nonlinear plan of action. Maybe you remember that I had failed to go on a university exchange program in the United States. Now I was trying to apply online for several internships over there, but my research proved unfruitful. I had no Social Security number (unique ID number in the United States). It was complicated to arrange such an internship from my student desk in France, and my American boyfriend couldn't help me either. I had to help myself and come up with a brilliant plan and soon.

Then I saw on Facebook that my Bulgarian high school friends were enrolling in summer work and travel student exchange programs in the United States via local Bulgarian agencies in conjunction with major American companies hiring students from countries with emerging or developing economies. I guess that this is why this type of exchange program is not popular in France and/or Western Europe.

United States, Work and Travel, A Lifeguard on Duty

The subsequent chain of events went like this: I arranged to fly back to Bulgaria for a few days and made an appointment with a local agency that put me in contact with CIEE, a nonprofit nongovernmental organization (NGO) leader in international student exchanges that had created the work and travel in the United States program sponsoring students to do summer internships and exchanges in the land where all your dreams come true.

After a brief conversation with the work and travel agent, I put a file together, and with the help of CIEE, I applied for an once-in-a-lifetime J1 visa. I was on my way to the United States, firstly in my mind and two months later for real. To Chicago, baby!

I was going to work as a lifeguard at a swimming pool and live in a nearby neighborhood, somewhere on the outskirts of Chicago. I wasn't about to turn lifeguarding into a career, but the program was a fantastic passage to the United States in a way that was legal and within the framework of a program. My parents paid for the flight about €450 ($494), and the new temporary structure took care of all the rest.

The local Chicago pool company introduced by CIEE arranged the accommodations and took care of the paperwork against the modest amount of about €450 ($494) to deal with all the hassle and faff. I thought it was a good deal. Also it is more secure and more prudent, in my opinion, to stick to a structure than wander around the world like a detached, clueless electron with no purpose, traveling without a cause. This time, I found a different type of program, which qualified and fit my criteria because it managed to provide me with a suitable structure adapted to my project.

Reciprocally, I also had to qualify to work as a lifeguard. I took an online course that lasted three days. This is how long the test was, and I actually had to study. On top of that, I had to do swimming exercises and tests in an indoor pool to prove my swimming skills. I grew up on the beach, deep-sea diving in the water throughout my entire childhood. One more skill that I had forgotten about until then: who would have thought it was going to link everything up so smoothly? It aligned perfectly with this master plan of mine.

Take life as if it were your playground. Where else can you test your abilities and capacity? Big deal if you fail, so what? You will learn from the mistakes. Remember that "only those who dare to fail greatly can ever achieve greatly" (Robert F. Kennedy). Chicago was the ideal spot for many reasons.

The Windy City was a well-known melting pot, very diverse with loads of opportunities in the media industry. Once on-site, my plan was to find a suitable internship in media, where I could learn firsthand and sponge knowledge while gaining credibility for my shiny curriculum-to-be. At that moment, I was just a wannabe wandering around the world, collecting valuable experiences and dear memories. I knew I was not marketable. I was not marketable in the way I wished and at the level I was targeting ... just not yet.

On my first day on duty as a lifeguard, I did an inventory of the situation and strategized on how to reorganize myself time-wise to make room for another project that had to be run simultaneously. The rather recreational activity I was exercising and treating as a source of income had to allow me somehow to attain my long-dreamed of internship in media in combination with my other passion, sun tanning at pool while doing my duty. This summer was raining a lot too, so I definitely had free time to occupy. I reset and focused myself.

After a few clicks on Craigslist, I finally found the perfect internship. I applied. The application was successful. I was about to start working for an affiliate film industry company of a major movie production giant. The internship was not paid, but at least I had access to free meals and could expense my public transport fees. It was good enough. You cannot have everything, right? The glass was half-full.

The plan was not over yet though. I needed additional income to sustain myself due to the lost income hours as lifeguard to the benefit of knowledge in the name of the professional media internship. I started working as a bartender in a fancy Japanese sushi restaurant in downtown Chicago, just a few blocks away from the skyscraper where I was completing my media internship. Everything was so well compacted. It was incredible. Even Mariya was impressed.

The structure I had produced was up and running in no time. It was a matter of weeks. The wheel was turning in the direction I wanted. I had managed to tick all the boxes I was there for. I didn't have to worry about where to live, as I was sharing a decent cheap flat together with two other foreign exchange lifeguards, located right next to the pool where we were working. Do you see the coincidence? Again, I was living next door to my job. There are no coincidences, though I do recommend you read chapter 2 and focus on the paragraph dedicated on how to organize yourself in respect to saving time by avoiding useless commuting.

To recap, my schedule was as follows: by covering the weekends lifeguarding shifts from 10:00 a.m. to 8:00 p.m., I had freed up most of my weekdays and dedicated my time from 9:00 a.m. to 5:00 p.m. to the media internship with the movie production company. From 6:00 p.m. to 12:00 a.m., I was bartending in the sushi restaurant. My journeys were carefully conceptualized and organized in the most compact way possible. A masterpiece, simply Mariya signature!

Chicago was also a specific target if you read later the Bulgaria episode. I mention the carefree childhood spent primarily on the beach. Along with the wicked summers, there were also some "Wicked Games" (inspired by Chris Isaak). The Bulgarian ex-boyfriend of mine featured in my version of "Wicked Games" was also living in Chicago at that moment. What a coincidence, right! Maybe secretly I wanted to check in on him. He happened to be on my way anyway, so I might as well liaise with him and announce my arrival right.

The time had come. We saw each other, but it meant nothing. Or it meant everything, depending on how you read it. Of course he had a girlfriend who lived in a different city who was coming to spend the summer with him in Chicago. The timing was spot-on. Do you see? The universe was obviously against this subconscious intention of mine.

In any event, the same thing that had pulled out the red carpet for M Basquite's plan to visit Uncle Sam's country had now taken away the red carpet. Something had aligned the planets to prevent any close encounters. The facts were staring me in the face, and I had to embrace them, suck it up, and redirect my energy elsewhere. I was still in touch with my on-and-off American boyfriend from Lyon. My whole life was an on-and-off basis, so it would make sense that my love life was not on track either. Can you guess the next twist that my life took? He turned up one random day in Chicago to surprise me. He was on an extended business trip, and this was for real, it wasn't orchestrated, not by him at least.

At the end of the summer, I was feeling at peace and most importantly satisfied with myself from the work done. I was ready to head back home to my lovely, cozy Lyon, to see my dear flatmates and friends, and to get back to work at the bar. Back to my safe paradise!

From Around the Globe

Episode: Mexico and Central America, Exchange Program

No pica. (It's not spicy.)

—A Mexican that is lying to you

Meanwhile Back in Lyon: Back to University and Back to the Bar

My summer adventure in the United States was over. I flew back to Lyon, and I was behind the bar, serving beer again. I had regained my favorite job, safe paradise, and comfort zone. The feeling was incredible. To be honest, I was happy and satisfied from my performance in the United States, but exhausted from all the adventures, I needed a break. I needed to recuperate before I embarked on the next unusual, exciting, and daring trip around the globe. I was about to go on the road again very soon, traveling around Central America this time, out of sunny Mexico, my base camp-to-be.

The time had come to reap the fruits from the actions I had taken before I left for Chicago. Remember, I wanted to learn Spanish. I informed you about this wish of mine in the episode dedicated to Brazil and South America. So I set an intention, backing it up with the right action, and then I waited patiently.

The action materialized in the form of an application to study abroad again. I had applied for Mexico this time. One random day after my shift at the bar, I received a phone call from the international relations department of my university in Lyon, telling me that I had been accepted to finish my M1 master's degree in Mexico. (Refer to chapter 7.) Moreover, I was going to be allocated three different, cumulable scholarships. To learn how to finance your project via scholarships, read chapter 8. Bingo! Simply Mariya!

By the look and feel of how fast things were moving, I knew that nothing could or should be taken for granted. I knew that this was the time to enjoy working at the bar and living in my cozy apartment. I realized I had to cherish every day being surrounded by wonderful people and life mentors. I was perfectly aligned with the time and space and was aware of it. I was living a lighthearted, easygoing student life, which I had designed myself. I was appreciative but attentive that this type of lightness may be temporary, so I did my best to enjoy every bit of the present moment.

In my naïve mind, upon reflection, I believed the universe had helped me orchestrate my Mexican project because I really had deserved and earned to have quality time off as well as enjoy the benefits of a full scholarship. I convinced myself that my sole purpose must be to be sent to Cancun, where I could relax and enjoy the pristine white sand and crystal-clear water the Caribbean Sea on Riviera Maya had to offer. My daydreams were often filled with all things around Mexico and the seemingly vivacious and exciting way of living in there.

My imagination, however, put me in the holiday mood, holidays which I could not afford. It had an enchanting effect on me all the same. The effect was so massive and powerful that it provoked a true desire to catapult myself to the beaches of Mexico. Run, Mexico!

I was about to embark on an extended studying holiday, funded by the French state, in the shape of the next student exchange program. Playful logic! Simply Mariya.

Can you guess what followed? Correct! My plan was sabotaged. One random day, I received a potentially life-changing phone call from my university international relations department, stating I was accepted to apply for an exchange program, but had to prepare and submit my application for Mexico. I needed extra help with the translation of all the documents into Spanish, but I hardly spoke any Spanish! How was I to overcome this obstacle, that is, to prepare the application form and then trigger the flow of financial resources packaged in a bundle of scholarships? So as not to temporarily sabotage your plans, read chapter 7.

This time the universe had arranged a competent figure to help me overcome this obstacle, conveniently located next door to my apartment. I rolled up my sleeves and knocked on the door of my extraordinarily smart South American neighbor for quality help using his skills as a highly educated native Spanish speaker. The solution was staring me in the face. It was a luxury. For the launch of this axe of my life project, I didn't need to traipse around sounding out a teacher from the faculty of Hispanic studies this time. Things seemed to be well laid out. My confidence was building again.

If I were Rachel Green, then this dude next door was a cultured version of Joey Tribiani. I trusted him. He knew this corner of the world better than I did and was able to give me good advice, or I thought so at least. I was running out of time. I had to work, go to school, and study for the approaching midterms. I was buried in documents in French and Spanish. To make it happen, I had to skip Google research (afterwards my focus was elsewhere). It was unthinkable as time was ticking away. Prioritize and skip some layers when you need to! I needed a little extra help to organize my choices, in the preparation of my next adventure that was already in the pipeline. You see how everything had melted together in my head. South America, North America and Central America equals Latin America. Same thing, right? Since Brazil is Lusophone speaking, it operates separately, but all Latinos must have good knowledge about their Spanish-speaking neighboring countries in Latin America, as they seem to operate together, right?! Sure, Mariya.

Based on the feedback of a friend of a friend, my dear well-informed neighbor recommended that I apply for a university located in Toluca de Lerdo. According to his description, he had heard from this friend of a friend that Toluca was supposed to be a charming, very picturesque student town, built in a neocolonial style with easy access to the beach. Technically I was sold on this imaginary place that the friend of a friend of a friend had strategically placed. (I bet you can see where this is heading.) It was somewhere near the beach in Mexico.

Guess what? I bought the idea straight away. I did not verify any of the facts or a single element of the discussion we had and filled in the paperwork by placing Toluca proudly as my first choice. Prioritize and skip some layers when needed!

One random day I received another cathartic phone call from the international divisions department congratulating me on my acceptance at the university in Toluca, Mexico, I ran and told my dear neighbor. I was ecstatic and had to share the big news. Beach and palm trees all for me, who wouldn't be restless in my shoes? I was about to go to the other side of the world. I had already had a taste of it during my adventures in Brazil, so I had tested the scheme. Me, myself, and I had already piloted the launch of Mariya in Brazil and loved it. I was grateful for this Mexican bonus. The second launch had to be spectacular.

I threw my arms around my friend's neck, squeezing his Latino cheeks and jumping up and down out of excitement. He invited me politely into his home and tried to calm me down. He had some more information to give me. He had made a mistake or had misunderstood his friend of a friend regarding all those good things he'd heard about the beaches in Toluca. Do you see the effect of *Le téléphone arabe* when applied in real life, when you make decisions and choices of importance based on stories heard through the grapevine?

Apparently Toluca was nowhere near the beach, but thankfully it was still in Mexico, as the university had confirmed my acceptance there. According to the updates, Toluca was right next to Mexico City. It was a small city, in Mexican terms, with a population of approximately 2.5 million people. It was industrial so tourists and exchange students tended to give priority to other corners of Mexico over Toluca. The Mexican connections back in Lyon had provided only this much information. Not much, I realized.

At the end of the day, did it really matter? This place was somewhere within the Mexican border, spoke Spanish, had Mexican music, and danced salsa, full stop. Worst-case scenario, I might have to travel to the beaches and explore out of the heart of the country. Many people would have had a hard time understanding how I could have underestimated such an important decision. I did not underestimate it though. I had to prioritize. Remember, I hadn't had the time to dedicate to research, and this wasn't an excuse for laziness. I was fully aware that I was leaving a small, tiny window in order to be surprised. I had to choose my battles. I had to choose wisely and at the speed of light as the international relations department was about to close the doors and Mariya would have missed the deadline! Gentle reminder, read chapter 7.

If I did not hurry, the project and all our joint effort would have gone down the drain as quickly as it had landed on my doorstep. Life is boring when you have everything planned down to the last detail and leave no chances for fate to perform. I like to occasionally leave a small window for the universe to wink at me. To do that, I knew I needed to leave a bit of room for correlation. I had a one-way ticket to a beach-less Toluca de Lerdo. It is almost sad to plan everything. As mentioned in chapter 1, life is a playground. I believe it and still practice this belief on regular basis.

The truth is that I didn't know when this crucial point occurred during the launch of the Mexico project. Since I was applying for my second exchange program, I had no priority over available spots. Other students who qualified to go abroad for the first time had the priority, like me once upon a time in Brazil. Right after I learned that there were no beaches in Toluca, I ran immediately to the international relations division to try to fix the hiccup. Yes, the sea is my timeless resource and one of my driving forces alongside languages. To manage to get to Mexico and be deprived of beaches was not my idea of fun. It sounded rather like a joke, one big prank.

I waited for hours at the door of the international relations division, desperately trying to swap places with someone who may want to exchange universities with me and respective cities. This was a no-go. Believe it or not, but based on what I observed and learned in the hours spent in front of this sacred holy office with magic powers, I came to realize that by unintentionally selecting Toluca, it being one of the very places in Mexico that had free spots to accommodate non-priority exchange students, I'd actually facilitated my application process. Hadn't I opted and focused on Toluca, moreover, having elected it as my preferred destination and first choice out of three possibilities, I don't want to think of the outcome. If I had not done so, I may never have qualified for the bonus exchange program, never lived near Central America, and never learned to speak Spanish. I will let you envisage the tremendous impact of this potential loss for someone with Mariya's drive to learn languages and travel around the globe. The consequences would have been devastating.

Luckily, the universe knows better and played in my favor and by the rules respecting *les règles de l'art* (the rules of art from French). I was confused. So there it was: the dawning realization that no one else would have put Toluca at the top of the list, meaning higher chances for me to be accepted. Good job, Mariya!

I had a hell of a time in Toluca. The cost of living was much cheaper, which directly translates into more trips, extended travels, and money to spend on clothes and presents for friends and familly. Could it be any better? It turned out to be the best choice ever! I was speaking Spanish almost fluently within the first month I arrived. Since I was surrounded exclusively by exchange students from Spain and Mexicans, I was fully immersed in a brand-new setting.

Toluca was located forty-five minutes away from the outskirts of Mexico City, when there is no traffic. When there is traffic, you can easily count a three-hour ride on a Mexican bus, watching high-end *telenovelas* (soap operas). Which is also fine, not that I was in a rush to go anywhere. I was on constructive holidays in sunny Mexico. And by the way, there were no palm trees in Toluca, but only pine trees and even snow on the top of the *Nevado de Toluca*, a volcanic mountain overlooking the city.

Climate-wise, it was probably the coldest place in the whole of Mexico. People-wise, it was probably the warmest place in Central America. There are indeed slight discrepancies between the way I visualized my Mexican dream, my expectations, and the way it all materialized. Did it really matter? Not to me. I was truly the happiest exchange student on the planet. I was more experienced post-Brazil. In Mexico, my experiences were amplified through close encounters with these exotic foreign lands, the native place of the mystical Mayas and Azteca.

I had built my lifelong projects against all odds, such as relocating to France to study with €1,000 ($1,096) in my pocket. Sounds like nonsense, right? I trust this is exactly how my undertakings looked from an external perspective, and quite frankly I was too busy to explain myself until now.

I was busy constructing the skeleton of this life template. Without knowing that Albert Einstein[13] had stolen my thunder by saying "Logic will get you from A to B. Imagination will take you everywhere," I can confirm that I was always guided by this mindset, and the proof is

---

[13] Albert Einstein (1879 – 1955) - a German-born theoretical physicist who developed the theory of relativity, one of the two pillars of modern physics, who received in 1921 a Nobel Prize in Physics" (Biography)

here. I fully relate to that principle, which I tested and put into practice myself without knowing that Uncle Einstein had already said it.

If someone's small little world or no matter the size does not generate imagination, I don't have a clue as to how they would acquire it, but maybe they can read this guide for inspiration, and it might trigger something inside of them.

Now I have the time I can iterate, clarify, analyze, and disclose this model of nonlinear thinking to you and demonstrate how I built the pillars of this entire text.

I am not going to bore you with all the stories from the numerous trips around Mexico, Guatemala, Cuba, and Panama. I will spare you the details of how I ended up trapped in a cave full of water along the Pacific Ocean by Puerto Escondido and keep the story of how we made it to Guatemala through the jungle for another time after being stuck at the Guatemala-Mexico border for several hours. I will let you follow me on Instagram if you wish to learn and see more about the Central American adventures cooked up by Mariya.

From Around the Globe

Episode: Paris, France. Sorbonne, Baby!

Paris is always a good idea.

—Audrey Hepburn[14]

Throughout my education process, I was introduced not only to the French culture, but also to the existence of the mythical University of the Sorbonne[15] in Paris, as I mentioned. I was doubly fascinated by this mesmerizing world of knowledge and concentration of intelligence that my teachers had explained to me back in high school. As you can guess, the Sorbonne was my next goal, or rather I was about to attempt my first goal after a 360-degree experience, depending on how you read it.

Shortly after I got back from Mexico, working at the bar downstairs and enjoying the time with my friends, I learned I had been accepted to study at the Sorbonne University. My dream had materialized, and I would have to leave again, this time for Paris, although I was distressed at not having enough time to reset, rethink, and benefit from the pleasure of my time in lovely, cozy Lyon. I wanted to spend time with my friends too. I had missed my comfort zone. I guessed

---

[14] Audrey Hepburn (1879 – 1955) - a British actress and humanitarian, also the first female actress to win an Oscar" (Biography)

[15] Sorbonne - established in 1257 in Paris, is the second oldest university in the history (Wikipedia) / Honoré de Balzac (1799–1850), French writer / Roland Barthes (1915–1980, literary critic, literary and social theorist, philosopher and semiotician / Simone de Beauvoir (1908–1986), French author, philosopher, and feminist

this was the price I had to pay to access a higher realm, to live such life-changing experiences. I attended the Sorbonne ("Paris is always a good idea") but learned that what mattered is the *voyage* ("trip" in English) in getting there, not the destination. I wanted to study in the Sorbonne University, like those philosophers I'd read about had done. Remember to set an intention! Like I did! I got accepted and paid a €5 ($5,5) tuition fee thanks to the scholarship system I used, described in chapter 8. The teachers were cherry-picked, and some of my teachers were teaching in Harvard. What and all for €5 ($5,5)?!

Trust me. It is all true. The tricky part was to get accepted in the legendary Sorbonne because here the selection was merciless. But hang on a moment! Look at my shiny, new CV that I'd built myself thanks to my social circle and my nonlinear mind that was tuned to detect good resources (e.g., knowledge, finances, and opportunities, but, most importantly, people).

Ironically, in the eyes of new people I met on my continuous journey, I realized that this made me come across like a privileged foreign student. This status then meant that my parents must be relatives of the Rockefellers. Or maybe my dad was the minister of finance back in Bulgaria and able to sponsor this bright and shiny CV (which was just a vitrine, but an important one).

On my first day at school, I was invited to a reception at the *Grands Salons de la Sorbonne,* or Sorbonne's big halls, a massive, elegant venue at Sorbonne's emblematic premises. I was surrounded by students, children of diplomats and/or ambassadors, and other personas from the Parisian high life, all dressed in Burberry and Louis Vuitton on the first day back at school, *la rentrée.*

Based on the inventory I just made for you and in respect of my new entourage, I immediately assumed that I would never make friends in this seemingly cold and pretentious place. Wrong! Sorbonne's imposing venues were cold indeed, but not the people.

During my first week, I made friends with four French girls. We had a special bond. The population of my major consisted of fifty percent foreigners; however for some reason I couldn't relate to the foreign students. I was feeling more comfortable and more at ease to live in a shared flat and hang out with my new French girlfriends. We helped each other with the emotional and financial resources we had to get through the midterms. Who would have expected that I would come across such a lovely, friendly group of Parisian girls? Why is nothing what it looks like? It would have been so much easier if there were a match between how things look versus their essence. I don't have the answer. I wish I could enlighten you, but I can tell you for sure that my classmates from the local university in cozy Lyon were nowhere nearly as friendly or ambitious as the kids I met in the cold environment of grandiose Sorbonne.

With my new group of friends, we hung out together and tried successfully to entertain ourselves in smart, low-budget ways. Next time, I will give you the names of all the hidden places and supply you with insights of Panam's ("Paris" in French slang) low-cost adventures. Only someone with the student status would know tips and tricks such as where to drink good, cheap beer for €3 per pint in central Paris while watching a live concert at the same time.

I bet you are wondering how I coped without a budget for the high living costs in Paris. Am I correct? Well, the student scholarships (read chapter 8) I kept benefitting from were definitely helping and giving me a good start and some stability. The "Caf" helped with the rent, but the state help was far insufficient. I was studying and working *en alternance*, which means I was doing professional internships simultaneously. Some of the days/weeks in the university's master's program were reserved for full day studies, and the rest of the time we had to validate half of our school performance through internships. The positive side of studying and doing internships is that according to the French legislation, companies have to remunerate students for working as interns for a period of over two months of employment.

I may say that finding an internship in Paris was one of the easiest tasks in my nonlinear life. I was very curious and uncertain as to how I would find a suitable internship that would fill out the Sorbonne's criteria's in order to qualify, but things just fell into place naturally. I was juggling internship after internship with university, having additional classes on Saturdays and running constantly to get to the next venue as the improvised classrooms were dispersed all over Paris. This inconvenience allowed me to get to know the City of Light like the back of my hand. There is always a bright side, right? I forgot to mention that at the beginning of the Parisian Sorbonne adventure, all students from my major were invited on a school trip to another famous European capital in a neighboring country, all expenses paid, but the flight ticket (which was more than affordable). Isn't that the best thing ever? Who would have guessed?

How can I ignore the fact that the universe was my friend and was looking after me with great care, making sure that my thirst to travel, learn, and sponge interesting facts was satisfied? I was always well served and able to constantly feed my imagination and curiosity. I couldn't always determine the destination I was swept to, but I was more than satisfied with the free school trip enabling me to visit over fifty museums, exhibitions, and tourist sites in one week. Was I born to see some of the world's most interesting pearls for free? What else was I supposed to think? Opportunities just kept popping up, and every move was fruitful to nonimaginable proportions. Why fret over a huge budget when life is so much more fun without it? Look how creative things can turn out!

Speaking of creativity, Disneyland is also one of the flagships of Paris and France. The luxury amusement park is often perceived as high-end kids' entertainment. Well, we were a bunch of grown-ups, ambitious kids who needed quality entertainment. So one of my Parisian friends piloted the weekend plans of how to take over and infiltrate Disneyland for free. Not only for free, but we were also honored with an upgrade to pass via the fast tracks, to gain time from queuing, and were given vouchers for free food on top. That's what I call high-end weekend treatment and quality entertainment with literally no budget, what undertook the equivalent to a five-star spa package in adult terms. Mind, body, and soul were riding those roller coasters in loop mode, full of light and happiness from the invention and the high standard production of this luxury weekend master plan at no cost.

This is how I believe we should look and treat the roller coaster of life, like a playground. You get to pick the playground. If it's going to be in your backyard or in Disneyland Paris (for free), it's up to you to decide. You are in control of it. In any event, there is no such thing as a free ride, only the illusion of it. The roller coasters at Disneyland were for free, but I had to make it to Disneyland and befriend intuitive people first to benefit from the full free-of-charge package. I had paid a price for it. The price was a lack of access to the pier at my favorite beach in my hometown. You can see how beautiful, peaceful, and relaxing this pier is in the Bulgaria episode.

One random day shortly after I graduated with reasonably high grades, thanks to the favorable soil in Paris, I had a revelation. I was no longer feeling fulfilled. I was feeling nostalgic for Lyon. I quit my job/internship in Paris and moved back to my shared flat above the bar, which my girlfriends had taken care of during my Paris getaway. I had my spot back, which materialized in the free sofa waving at me to come home. I got my job back as a bartender at the bar downstairs. Call it law of attraction or force of attraction, but I needed to reset my mind, to rethink and strategize the next move before the wheel started turning again. The best and safest place to do that was of course Lyon, the base of where everything had started. In a way, I saw the base I had built in Lyon as the mother ship. When I needed to reset or think quietly in a safe, happy place, the mother ship in Lyon called me.

From Around the Globe

Episode: Switzerland, Lake Life

What's the biggest plus about living in Switzerland? Well, the flag is a big plus.

—Roger Federer[16]

After my Parisian stopover, I returned to Lyon, back to my safe paradise. I rolled up my sleeves and got back to work at the bar. My flatmates and friends were still there. We hosted couch surfers occasionally so we could maintain our running costs and the monthly rent. The flexibility of this scheme allowed me to maintain for many years the floating structure I had built piece by piece. My entourage was of course also benefitting from the small advantages I'd fabricated for us. Most importantly, I had permanent access to a stable, safe place, connected to a network of down-to-earth people I could hold on to when the roller coaster of life shook up.

Simultaneously I had spent months trying to fix my relationship with my on-and-off American boyfriend who was still based in Lyon. During the episode in Paris, he happened to be there for work a lot, and again due to or thanks to work-related circumstances, we got to spend some time together. Again it was not orchestrated, not by him at least. I had to recognize the fact that our connection was strong.

All roads led me back to Lyon, so here I was, back in the game, serving beer in one of my favorite places on earth. This was a short-term solution though as the core idea was to

16 Roger Federer (1981) - a Swiss professional tennis player, who has won 20 Grand Slam men's singles titles" (Biography)

make use of and monetize this shiny, new CV of mine. I had put so much effort into building it and polishing it nicely. The search for a corporate job, however, was proving difficult. I wasn't going in the right direction for some reason. For the first time I was experiencing what I like to call the effects of "all doors shut." I had to identify and understand the reason(s) for this unpredicted situation ASAP.

In the meantime, I was bartending and using my downtime to apply for jobs and gain interviews with companies who appeared intimidated by the profile I had carefully designed. It was not the outcome I had pictured at all. Admiration is not a synonym of intimidation. The repercussions from these types of discrepancies could be huge. Something was off or had gone wrong, and/or I had underestimated something. I was investigating all kinds of options and directions in and around Lyon to enable me to finally join this divine corporate world and get that lucrative high-profile job that I had long dreamed of. The outcome of my search was not successful. I was devastated; my project had a leak. That's not how Mariya works!

One random evening, however, I went to a birthday party. Here I met a lady who provided an answer to my leak: I was in the wrong location. The unique profile I had tailored, along with the pile of languages I spoke, was more than marketable in a country like neighboring Switzerland, which is also unique. I went back home, and after a few random clicks, my CV and cover letter were on their way to the *Suisse voisine*. Of course, there is no such thing as random, as we have seen and as I have proved so far.

The very next day I received a phone call from an unknown number. I was invited to interview with a high-profile international company in the industry I always dreamed of being a part of. I could totally picture myself joining this mesmerizing new world that I was being invited in to. The news was big, it was so big, and I was jumping up and down like a child and again squeezing the Latino cheeks of my friend, colleague and fellow neighbor, who had sent me to adventurous Toluca in Mexico a few years before.

The interview went well. Finally the leak was no longer a leak. It was an upgrade I had not foreseen. Why hadn't I predicted or anticipated it? Well, because behind the ambitious vitrine, I secretly wanted to get a down-to-earth corporate job, yet remain living in lovely, cozy Lyon, happily ever after enjoying the time with my cherry-picked entourage of friends. My vision was evolving in one direction, but my path was pointing in another. I dare to question why things cannot simply be aligned, clear, and more linear just for once. Not on Mariya's journey apparently.

I accepted the job offer and moved to work in Switzerland. The job was worth it; the professional setting was outstanding. The quality of human resources Switzerland had attracted and cherry-picked was extraordinary. Each invitee of the Helvetic Confederation was there for a specific reason and gifted in their own way. People had a purpose; some had higher purposes. What was mine? What do you think?

Contrary to what I expected, my performance was good, but not brilliant. The structure I was dealing with was unbreakable and inflexible and with sturdy, well-grounded pillars that even Mariya couldn't shake up or restructure. When I say "shake up," I mean it in a positive, progressive way, as I naturally tend to look for potential opportunities to implement an upgrade in a nonlinear manner, to improve things, and I see this in every problematic situation.

I soon befriended this rather cold, serious, almost sterile environment. The almost-clinical ambience was very different compared to the warmth of my life back in Lyon where everybody knew my name.

Regardless, in a matter of months, Switzerland turned into a happy yet temporary place. The scenery in this country is breathtaking. I took advantage of lake life that so many people who live there do. The relaxed weekends coupled with some mountain adventures were like a breath of fresh air compared to the extremely busy workdays. I strongly recommend checking out this rare pearl in the middle of Europe, offering some of the most unique landscapes on earth. Nevertheless, the temporary feeling never left my mind or heart.

Unfortunately I am not able to disclose much, if anything, about my fascinating professional life in Switzerland due to confidentiality. In order to remain secret, I prefer to keep the multitude of stories to myself and apologize to my readers for depriving you of one of the most exciting parts of Mariya's journal.

However, the time had come. After six wonderful years spent in stunning Switzerland, I felt like London was calling me. I was getting tired of all the moving, and I realized it was high time to finally settle. Exhausted from constantly running after the next opportunity that is not necessarily correlated to the right location, I recognized London as the place to settle. I had to think and be honest with myself. I can tell you now that London had never been in my sights. However, I couldn't disregard the fact that this megapolis located culturally and geographically between the United States and Europe was a true island of opportunities offering a perfect ecosystem I believed was the solution. The dense concentration of job offers in the industry I was experienced in made the move even more appealing and appeared as a low-risk destination. Pay attention to the word "appeared," and you will learn why in the next episode, "London's Calling."

The time had come. The decision was taken. I was about to move to London, baby! It was just a matter of time. However, on the last day of work, I had joined my dear workmates on a team building event in an exquisite mountain resort in the French Alps. How could I possibly miss out on the opportunity to hang out with my friends and deprive myself from an extra day in the breathtaking Alps? Well, I didn't, and guess what? Of course, what else could happen to Mariya that follows the rule of new chapters that are attained against all odds? The sky was crystal-clear with top visibility that any skier would appreciate, and the snow conditions were beautiful with fresh powder all for me. Now was the time to jump on my very last ride and hit those steep Alpine slopes. Before I knew it, bam! Five kilometers into a thirty-five kilometer-long wall-like steep slope, I took one wrong move, and the consequence was announced before me—broken cruciate ligaments, resulting in a true bang, a proper explosion, and a hanging kneecap that called for medical intervention. Long story short, the operation took place in a five-star hospital with a sensational view toward the Lake Léman that I couldn't have cared less about it.

So the London project was on hold, and my familiar life back in France was calling me. Yup, my long-term friend and part of the diasporas of flatmates from the student years spent in the flat above the bar came to the rescue. Mariya was riding back to Lyon, feeling like precious cargo on the back seat and saying goodbye to the lovely Lake Léman and the steep mountains, cargo on crutches.

Repaired after the ski adventure in a high-end Swiss lake view resort—sorry, I meant lake-view hospital—I was back in Lyon where my friends took care of their grumpy, injured guest on rotation. My plans hadn't completely gone down the drain yet. I was still convinced and determined that I needed to make it to London.

From Around the Globe

Episode: United Kingdom, London's Calling

When a man is tired of London, he is tired of life.

—Samuel Johnson[17]

Basing myself in London finally gave me all the time I needed to rethink, reset, and re-strategize and to put all of my knowledge, insights, and adventures in writing. Making it to London on crutches gave me the opportunity to communicate. There was no more Latin-American dancing for a while and no skiing or jogging in the parks all over green London. I used this time to fine-tune myself into finding the right job and to prepare this book for you. I insist on sharing one sentiment of mine with you that maybe some of you reading these words have already come across.

What I experienced in London is a common feeling like the moment that many bright people with undiscovered potential have experienced, including *Harry Potter* author J. K. Rowling, for example. I call this the all-doors-shut momentum. J. K. Rowling had this continuous idea of a story of a specially gifted boy with a magical wand that the world fell in love with. She kept hold of her story, but she finally focused and started writing it only when all doors were shut.

I knocked on many doors and listened to a great number of important decision-makers from the corporate world in supposedly progressively thinking London. The outcome was

---

[17] Samuel Johnson (1709 – 1784) - an English writer and creator of the Dictionary of the English Language" (Biography)

always the same. My CV was either scrutinized under a monocle. The content and format was often perceived as rather interesting but a bit unusual though—unusual ... hmm, really—or people hardly looked at it.

On many occasions, I sat face-to-face with an authority from an imposing and well-known international company based in London, but because Human Resources had arranged the meeting, the people before me hadn't bothered to look at the sheet on their desk prior to our appointment. I was continuously given the chance to proceed to the next irrelevant discussion with an executive or a VP, thanks to the spider web of HR systems in London and a lack of help from the universe in finding me the dream job.

For some unknown, illogical, mystical reason, the discussions and ideas obtained during the one-to-one conversations never materialized into anything concrete. I had pre-arranged to have quality time and resources available through this episode. As a true workaholic, I was not satisfied from my performance. I wasn't seeing anything brilliant so far. I was convinced I was built to reproduce structures, convey messages, and simply deliver. My communist-influenced upbringing was speaking, I was sure.

Since no employer had given me the green light, I had no carte blanche to take care of their project. So I designed my own. Here I was finally able to reset and center my thoughts on this book. I hope you find my thoughts interesting and see the provided template as a keeper. As I said in the beginning of my journey in chapter 1, my intention and real purpose behind this book is to firstly reassure parents to let their young adults go and, secondly, provide proof that you as a young adult should not get obstructed by a lack of money and tell you not to be afraid to explore and exploit your own resources. I hope to motivate and inspire young adults with big ambitions and unrealistic dreams to break the chains of social boundaries, to go on a constructive journey built in a smart way and enjoy the ride that life is offering. Don't be afraid if things seem unapproachable or far from your grasp. Don't be afraid of the unknown, but don't be careless either. Remain disciplined, keep hold of your awareness, and life will be generous with you.

I like to believe that I have been purposely empowered with the necessary free time and sturdy financial resources required to write this book. The big plus on the Swiss flag was waving at me, and the London vibe helped me to find inspiration to compile all of this sturdy information in the chapters and stories I organized in the episodes. I decided to accept the current situation I found myself in and perceived it as a red carpet that someone had rolled out for me to write and share this life template with you.

Why refer to it as the red carpet? Because life arranged an abundance of three crucial pillars that enabled me to produce this portal for future generations. I kept this content in my own personal cloud, where no one had access to it but me. From an outside view obviously, I had taken the monopole over the work and travel student exchange programs because it is that easy to do these things out of France, but the truth is that it isn't. I was finding lame excuses and procrastinating in typing that novel, but I finally found time to demystify how to do brilliant things with no budget. An incentive arrived that made me get a grip on the precious time I was misusing. The notion of time is, I would say, pillar number one.

1. Time flies and doesn't come back.

2. Health is vital and very precious.

3. Of course we can't do much without capital (money) when time, our most precious asset, is carved out of our asset library.

Do you see this catch-22 scenario? At least this is how I read it. I needed time to organize, conceptualize, structure, and write this life essay, and I had earned the money that enabled me to do so. I wish to believe that the next wave of book-smart and street-smart kids may find it useful to build their life story using my competition format following the hints, tips, and tricks I discovered sometimes the hard way. Yes, life is a constant competition and has different formats. You are just being introduced to one type of format, Mariya's.

When someone with a shiny CV and a good profile comes from a diverse background experiences, the effect of all doors shut, as J. K. Rowling had encountered, I dared to believe it was destiny, allowing me to give you, the next generation, what I was given, information for the sole purpose of triggering your own abundance of opportunities via my tips and tricks to a higher realm, to a higher purpose.

In my endeavors, I follow simple universal rules as you may have noticed. All these elements are secondary to common sense; however as demonstrated on several occasions, specific events were calculated, and decisions were made and prioritized differently in order to provoke a specific, almost-automated flow of positive circumstances. But what if "common sense is not so common" (Voltaire)?

My advice is not to get distracted by fake opportunities yet go with the flow as I have explained to you. Learn to identify scams and time-wasting activities. Identify what is real and then learn to give back. I hope I'm giving my readers an inspiring story full of gratitude, positive vibes, and moral lessons, but most importantly sturdy knowledge and real-life insights ready to use and apply to build your own dream project.

It is important to take a step back and analyze and acknowledge our failures because they are inevitable. The key is to acknowledge them. Take a moment and a deep breath. Be honest with yourself and try to identify why you believe you have failed. Try to be in a light, playful mindset when you do this exercise, as you might discover that the universe had arranged things in a better way for you and has access to greater knowledge then we have.

To give you a concrete example, look at my adventure in Mexico. It is proof of failure with a happy ending, which presented in a logical way should be classified and judged as high-end sabotage of my master plan, plotted by my dear next-door neighbor for reasons beyond my knowing. Logic often limits us. What is the definition of logic? "Reasoning conducted or assessed according to strict principles of validity," as Oxford's dictionary presents. But who validated those principles?

The best argument society invented is to teach each other how to kill the ideas, dreams, and ambitions of others by learning to state and emphasize that of what your comrade is doing and claiming aloud that it has no logic, full stop. What about if your comrades have discovered a different, better logic than the one thought out by society, a society full of well-established boundaries and a shiny, fabricated vitrine?

Look at this shiny vitrine. Look at what is actually behind it. Do you see my logic and what I mean now? Does it work better to challenge your nonlinear mind and soul to work in your opinion than to follow the common linear logic? I will let you be the judge.

I hope I have motivated you in some way to follow your ambitions and unrealistic dreams, to prove that anything is possible if you believe in it enough. I am currently based in London, and if you wish to learn more tips and tricks and read about my next adventure, join me on social media and follow me on Instagram. I will soon be broadcasting my new escapades out of trendy London. I might be less active sometimes, but meanwhile I finally got the dream job in the most mesmerizing industry, known as the Fourth Estate.

What's next? See on *mariya_atg* on Instagram. I hope you enjoyed the read! I look forward to hearing from you soon.

With best regards,

Mariya

From Around the Globe

Episode: Bulgaria, Beach Time

Everything, far from the sea, is province.

—Ernest Hemingway[18]

I was born in Bulgaria in a seaside city located on the Black Sea and knows as the Sea capital of the country. Speaking of the Black Sea, I swear I still have flashbacks nourished by the memories of my happy childhood. Various vivid images keep swirling through my mind even nowadays, of those unique moments spent on the beach a ten-minute walk from my parents' house.

I remember with warmth those long, hot summers coupled with playful games with my childhood friends. We were gifted with the chance and natural aptitude to do silly things. Armed with great talent and imagination, we always found the means to deliver a mischievous project created to annoy parents, teachers, and any grown and responsible thinking individual concerned with the next idea that we were devising.

First Encounter with the French

My school friends and I spent carefree years running around the pristine beaches in Bulgaria. Years went by, and one random day during the summer holidays, I met a group of French guys on the beach who were there on an exchange program. I had no knowledge of what an exchange program entailed, but the concept nonetheless intrigued me. As a curious youngster, I kept

---

[18] Ernest Hemingway (1899 – 1961) - an American journalist, novelist, short-story writer, and sportsman, won a Pulitzer Prize for Fiction (1953) and a Nobel Prize in Literature (1954)" (Biography)

this notion in mind just in case I came across such an opportunity at a later undetermined stage in my life. This random encounter with cute French guys triggered my interest about the country, culture, and possibilities that this foreign land seemed to offer. I felt the physical urge to explore further. These guys represented a true source of inspiration and motivated me to make it to France when the right time came around and perhaps even meet them again on their own territory.

I cherished every day spent in their company, not only because they were, to me, exotic, but also because they were smart and knowledgeable and had a clear vision of what they wanted to do, where they wanted to be, and how to get there once they were done with their Bulgarian summer exchange adventure. They had a new methodology, new to me.

The independence they had captivated me, and naturally I wanted the same access to studies and freedom as them. I knew immediately that, regardless of the topics, I was going to study in France. Again, remember to set an intention! It is useful, and now you see why.

Gallery

From Around the Globe

Man cannot discover new oceans unless he has the courage to lose sight of the shore.

—Andre Paul Guillaume Gide[19]

Voyage, voyage ("a trip" or "a journey" in English), What matters is the *voyage*, not the destination!

***Mail on Sunday*, British Journal**

One random day during my lunch shift at the bar in Lyon (on the map above), a group of journalists approached me because they were working in Lyon on an inquiry, the first face transplant in the world. The face in question was that of a French lady who had tried to commit a suicide by taking an overdose. After having passed out from the overdose, her dog had disfigured her face while trying to resuscitate her. The story itself, in conjunction with the first esthetical surgical operation involving a face transplant, had attracted many famous tabloids to Lyon. The *Mail on Sunday* temporarily recruited me as a French-English translator and interpreter. My mission involved helping them navigate their efforts to reach out to glorified key esthetical surgeons, lawyers, the victim herself, and the other secondary parties that were taking part in the story.

This first real job allowed me to get close insights of the lifestyle of a journalist and see the methodology they use to get to the content they are hired to write about. I had been given

---

[19] Andre Paul Guillaume Gide (1869 – 1951) - a French author and winner of the Nobel Prize in Literature (in 1947)" (Biography)

direct access to learn from the exciting context and environment I was parachuted in to. I was observing firsthand the maneuvers the journalists were using to liaise with the right individuals at the right time in order to write in a holistic way about the macabre story.

I wasn't only given exposure to what it actually meant to be a journalist, but I was also given the opportunity to exercise my multiple language skills for the first time in a professional setting. I was given carte blanche to make direct use of what I had learned over the years, and more importantly I ended up getting paid a significant amount of British pounds for my translation services. The cash I earned with sweat was converted/invested into a travel plan and a flight ticket to Togo in West Africa.

West Africa: First Experience outside of Europe

I was still in touch with the French friends I'd met on the beach back in Bulgaria. With some being from African descent, I shared with my friend this intrigue of mine to go on a trip to a remote destination outside of Europe and start exploring the world. I was offered to join the trip to Togo the following summer. I was delighted by the idea and immediately accepted to be part of the adventure.

We met at Orly Airport in Paris. After staring at the flight timetable waiting for our gate, it was announced that there was a slight delay in the takeoff due to technical issues. We had purchased the cheapest tickets we could find, which were with Air Burkina. The airline doesn't exist anymore luckily; however back in those days, Air Burkina was on the blacklist of the airline companies and for obvious reasons. After being offered food and hotel vouchers, several hours later we were informed that we could embark on the next flight to Bamako, Mali, instead. Once in Bamako, we were to change flights to Lomé, Togo.

After landing in Mali, it was announced that there were no more direct flights to Togo that day. Therefore, we were offered to remain seated on the same plane, which was continuing its journey to Ouagadougou in Burkina Faso, which was closer to our final destination. So eleven passengers, including my friend and me, remained onboard the flight, which took us to Ouagadougou instead. We landed safely at 4:00 a.m. in a country that I could not have located on a map. All I knew is that we were closer distance-wise to our final destination.

At custom control, however, I was told that I was not allowed to leave the transit zone because I had no visa, which was required for Bulgarian citizens entering the country. I was stuck in the flight connection zone for an indeterminate amount of time. I was unprepared for this, and my motivation was declining rapidly, but how could I have anticipated such an incredibly random, unexpected circumstance?

Who would have thought something like this could happen in real life? I was starting to feel that my life was going to be full of adventures, but at that very moment it was too much to bear. My friend spoke to the police control, and somehow I was supplied with an unordinary trespassing visa, which enabled me to leave the airport. We were told that the airport did not know when the next flight from Ouagadougou to Lomé was scheduled, but they assured us that it would happen and that we needed to remain patient.

All eleven passengers were sent to the best hotel in the capital, which in my opinion was equivalent to a one-star motel according to French standards. There was no hot water in the room, and the TV had five channels with the poorest feed and content quality. The group from Paris stayed in the hotel for the entire three days until the next flight to Lomé was organized. Meanwhile, a petition was quickly prepared and signed, and the French embassy was informed that our group was stuck in no-man's-land for unknown period.

We stayed in Ouagadougou for the next three days and then travelled to Lomé. The capital of Togo was a strange place for Mariya, but strange in a good way. We travelled through the country together and experienced the African lifestyle in the most authentic way. Actually I will let you discover Togo, if you are interested, via all the travel blogs available on the web and my visual materials that can be found *where*? Well, *mariya_atg* on Instagram!

But this story is not about Togo or any of my other trips around the globe. This story is about unique moments that presented themselves in a nonlinear life, experienced and documented through the eyes of an adventurer. After my trip to the francophone part of Africa, I returned to Lyon safely and once again regained the normality of life.

Epilogue

In a nutshell, I have showcased some concepts and methods, provided concrete guidelines, and shared precious episodes of a true story. I have chronicled this chain of events to motivate you to build your own life project. Let's assume that you are not interested in studying in the Sorbonne in Paris, but you love pasta and want to study at in Italy, but then might have to reconsider your choice as the Bocconi university in Milan would cost you much more than 5€ tuition fees per year. Also maybe you're not fond of the beach but prefer the mountains. It does not matter because both the concept and methodology remain the same, while the main focus is for you to find inspiration and motivation all the same.

I hope I have demonstrated how to be bold, to believe in yourself, to trust your intuition, and to hold on to your dreams until they turn into reality because anything is possible when you want it with your heart, mind, and soul while money is just an accessory.

I hope you enjoyed the read!

Thank you and best wishes,

Mariya

Printed in the United States
By Bookmasters